PROPERTY INVESTING FOR DOCTORS

PROVEN STRATEGIES FOR BUSY PROFESSIONALS

DR LAFINA DIAMANDIS

Property Investing for Doctors

First published in December 2018 by Eurekadoc Publishing
Eurekadoc LLP, 27 Old Gloucester Street, Bloomsbury, London WC1N 3AX
property@eurekadoc.com www.eurekadoc.com

This book is available online and in book stores.

A catalogue record for this book is available from the British Library.

Cover design Kostis Pavlou.

Front cover photograph: Tarun Ram.

Back cover photograph: Yolande de Vries Photography.

CONTENTS

INTRODUCTION

Most of us are too busy working to pay attention to our financial health—especially us doctors and medical students. Often, we don't know where to start or who to trust. We're inexperienced when it comes to money matters, and sometimes downright naïve due to our trusting nature and the non-profit driven environment in which we work.

Maybe you want to buy your own home, invest in a cash-flowing asset or set up a healthcare service. Whatever your plans, this book will give you a solid foundation of knowledge on which you can build over time. It addresses essential investment principles and strategies, as well as how to deal with the most common challenges in property, such as funding your investment, choosing a builder or managing your property. Hopefully, what you'll learn in this book will also protect you against any sharks in the investment world!

This book is suitable for complete beginners to experienced investors. It will help medical students (and their parents!) looking for a way to fund accommodation expenses for the next five to seven years, doctors with zero geographical stability (thanks to hospital rotations requiring them to move from one area to another) who might be struggling with the decision of where to buy, locum doctors struggling to get a mortgage due to insufficient proof of income, and consultants looking for ways to boost cash flow, make their savings work harder or maximise their pension.

You might be one of those creative, entrepreneurial and ambitious doctors out there, someone who runs a business or needs some property knowledge. And perhaps you're time poor and cash-strapped. I want to share what I've learned with some of the most talented, hard-working and altruistic individuals in society. That's you.

Although the strategies in this book are based on my experience in the UK, they can be used anywhere in the world. However, you will need to consider differences in legal systems relating to obtaining finance and taxation. For example, Scotland has different rules and regulations to England and Wales when it comes to property (for example, stamp duty and land tax rates differ), so you'll need to seek legal and financial advice if you want to invest in Scotland.

All effort has been made to provide accurate and up to date information, and I am sharing information and strategies I have used, observed or learnt myself. Of course, these strategies and information are reflective of the current property market and may be subject to change in the future. Be aware that I'm not a financial advisor and the content in this book is shared for educational purposes only. You should always seek the advice of an appropriately qualified professional regarding any investment decisions. I hope you'll enjoy reading this book as much as I've enjoyed writing it, and if you have any suggestions for how this book could be improved for future editions, or you spot something that requires further clarification, I would love to hear from you at: property@eurekadoc.com.

I'm interested in property investment but where do I start?

It can feel overwhelming when you start out and don't know whether property investing is for you, where to invest, which strategy to use or how to choose the right property. Below are eight steps you can use to approach property investment and explore whether property investment is right for you and what is likely to be involved.

Why do you want to invest?

What is of paramount importance is that you clarify your own reasons for investing in property. That means you will need to invest time and effort in developing the skills, knowledge and network you need to succeed. Therefore, it must be worth your effort and precious time. Thankfully, this doesn't take anywhere near as long as it takes to become a doctor! If you're extremely driven, it's possible to have your first investment up and running within thirty days. Being more realistic, you should give yourself six to twelve months. It's a good idea to write down your top three reasons for investing in property so you can assess how important they are to you and how they fit with your personal, professional and financial goals.

What are your goals?

Once you're clear why you want to get into property investment, set goals for the next six, twelve and eighteen months (or perhaps you prefer one, three or five year goals). Think about setting personal, professional and financial goals and visualise how your life will be when you achieve them. Some people find a vision board helpful (a collage of images that represents your goals). Ask yourself whether property investment will help you achieve any of those goals.

Get educated!

Like with any new interest, you'll need to develop skills in and knowledge about property investment. Otherwise, how will you know how to invest, where to invest and what sort of properties to invest in? There's a multitude of books, webinars and courses available, as well as some fantastic property networking meetings all over the UK. Make sure you read widely and use all the resources available to you.

Prepare yourself

Once you feel confident in your knowledge and have a strategy in mind, you should prepare yourself to invest and get ready for your first deal. One way of doing that is thinking about the resources you will need—people, funds, knowledge, skills and experience. Getting prepared includes putting your team of professionals in place so they can help you achieve your goals (solicitor, accountant, mortgage broker, handyman, builder). If you don't have contacts already, don't panic. No one does at the start. Make a list of who you'll need to help you and ask friends and contacts for recommendations. Reach out to those recommended so you have the connections ready to go when the time comes. You may also need to prepare yourself financially by ensuring you have a suitable credit score and report and tidy up any undesirable spending habits! You can view my free module at: Preparing to Invest at: www.eurekadoc.com/preparing-to-invest.

Choose your strategy

Choose a strategy that will help you to reach your goals. Your strategies may change over time. That's OK, as the most important thing is to choose one and focus on it. Investing in property can feel exciting in the beginning, and many people try to do too much at once. This makes it difficult to achieve what you want, as you use more energy finding and analysing different property projects making it harder to scale and systemise your business. (My own strategy has changed a lot over the years.)

Find your first project

Finding that first deal is always the hardest, but once you've got it the rest will come. The more specific and narrow your criteria, the easier it will be to find a deal. Deciding on your personal criteria for investment will make it easier to filter out noise and distractions from properties that don't fit your strategy. Once you find your ideal investment, and have your offer accepted, make sure you see the purchase through to completion. Regular communication with agents, solicitors and broker may be required, so be sure to stay in the loop with what is going on both to protect your deal as well as demonstrate consistency and reliability.

Funding your project

Once you've decided on your property strategy and know what kind of property to look for (and how to find it), have your funds ready. The earlier you can secure funds for your project, the better. Ideally you should organise and secure the funds for your project before you have even found the property. If you have funds ready (including a mortgage offer, if applicable) you'll appear as a stronger buyer and this could make all the difference in a competitive market.

Systemise your property business

Once you've invested in your first property, you need to think about how best to streamline it. Everything from paying your expenses to finding tenants to maintenance and accounting should be considered, and (where possible) systemised and outsourced. This might include refurbishment, letting and managing your property, bookkeeping and more. Being a doctor is busy enough, and the last thing you want is to create another full-time job for yourself as a property manager!

I hope these eight steps have given you an idea of where to start when you approach investment. You are already taking a step in the right direction by reading this book.

CHAPTER 1

WHY DOCTORS SHOULD INVEST IN PROPERTY

There are lots of reasons why you might want to invest in property, and some of those reasons will be common to the general population. However, there are factors specific to us doctors that make investing in property a no-brainer. A doctor's life is pretty tough and the purse strings can be tight, so consider this book a value-add, designed to provide you with some home truths and hopefully a financial health boost! Doctors love lists, so here are my reasons why investing in property is a good idea for doctors and medical students and their families.

To solve our accommodation dilemmas

Whether you're a medical student or consultant, putting a roof over your head (and of those you love) can involve considerable financial expense. Medical students not living at home (or their parents) are faced with paying large sums in rent every year for five to seven years. Junior doctors who frequently move areas for rotations often feel too unsettled to make a long-term residential purchase decision, but they could take advantage of short-term property investments that offer the flexibility they need until they're ready to buy their own home. Consultants may have different housing needs, such as providing for a family, covering the cost of a mortgage or wanting to invest in property in the long-term. Investing in property can be a great way to cover your accommodation needs as well as generate extra income or act as a valuable long-term asset. And there are ways to do this without requiring huge lump sums or actually purchasing a property.

To generate income to cover the cost of training as well as lifestyle choices

Medical training is one of the longest and most expensive training programmes around, and income generated from property investment can go a long way towards supporting both postgraduate and undergraduate training costs as well as everyday expenses. It is never too early (or too late) to invest in property.

Medical students

The cost of becoming a doctor in the UK is higher than ever before. The average UK medical student needs a minimum budget of £20,000 per year thanks to the government hiking up fees—and rents are rising, too! That's £100,000 for a five-year university course; you could buy a property for the same amount (even several) in some parts of the UK.

Junior doctors

Unfortunately, when it comes to the expense of education and training, the buck (quite literally) doesn't stop after finals. It can be a shock when you realise that with the title 'Dr' you suddenly acquire all sorts of expenses you hadn't realised you'd be spending your hard earned (and long awaited) cash on! Some junior doctors, particularly following the contract changes last year, have found themselves in dire straits. For anyone unfamiliar with UK postgraduate medical training expenses, here are a few examples of annual costs we are obliged to pay:

GMC registration: £420 per year

Medical indemnity insurance: £80 - £2,000 per year

Medical courses: £400 - £2,000 per course

Royal College memberships: (for example, for e-portfolios, publications that sit unread on the coffee table for months) £300 upwards

Royal College exam fees: £200 - £1,500 per exam

Subscriptions and memberships: (variable)

Contrast the above costs with your friends from other fields (many will get training courses and exam expenses paid, not to mention weeks off for study leave) and it seems like an uneven playing field! Most junior doctors in training will earn around £2,000 per calendar month for the first five years after qualifying (F1–ST3). If you decide to become a GP, you're looking at five years of the average UK salary, and if you decide on becoming a speciality consultant (eight to ten years of training in total), your salary will rise incrementally—but don't forget you will be taxed 40% on everything you earn over £46,350 per annum (as of 2018). Being able to generate different streams of income will serve you well in your junior doctor years and beyond.

Consultants and GPs

Most consultants and GPs I meet are interested in property investment as a means of generating extra income to pay for mortgages, support dependants, and support their lifestyle choices. GPs in particular often have to self-fund expensive medical indemnity insurance. Most senior doctors are higher rate tax payers whose monthly income after tax may not be enough to cover their personal and professional expenses. They want their hard-earned cash to start to work harder for them and property investment can certainly do this.

Investing in property as early as possible (ideally from when you're a medical student) means you can benefit from:

Capital appreciation of your property over the period of your medical training and career.

Earning up to £7,500 tax free income per annum from renting a room in your home to a lodger—this may cover your accommodation expenses.[1]

1 HM Revenue & Customs, 'Rent a room in your home' https://www.gov.uk/rent-room-in-your-home/the-rent-a-room-scheme [accessed 11th November, 2018].

Generating high cash flow by renting several rooms in a house (a multi-let) and using the income to cover your living costs and generate savings.

Earning tax free income up to £11,850 if you have no other income source (as of 2018).

Developing business skills and getting landlord experience.

Note that if your parents are planning on buying a property (in their own names) for you to live in while at university, and want to transfer it to you at a later date, you could be liable for Inheritance Tax (IHT) and Capital Gains Tax (CGT). Inheritance Tax is the tax payable on the estate of someone who has died and amounts to 40% on the value of the estate that is over the threshold of £325,000. Capital Gains Tax is payable on gains from residential property (second homes or investments) but is not payable if you sell the home that you are living in. If you're a higher rate tax payer, you will pay 28% on your gains from residential property. If you're a basic rate tax payer, the rate payable depends on the size of your gain and your other taxable income.

Depending on your personal situation, it may be worth your parents helping you to buy the property in your own name instead by acting as guarantors for the mortgage. This means that if you use the home as your primary and main dwelling, and sell the property at a later date, you will not be liable for CGT or IHT.

Capital appreciation example

Assuming you buy a property for £200,000 and the capital appreciation is 5% per year, the values would be as follows:

Year 1	£200,000
Year 2	£210,000
Year 3	£220,500
Year 4	£231,525
Year 5	£243,101
Year 6	£255,256

The profit from capital appreciation alone over a six-year period is £55,256, and if you consider the further income you could make through renting out a spare room (or multiple rooms) in your property, investing in a property can be a wise and profitable investment.

Property investment can support flexible working and diverse career paths

Making ends meet can be even more of a challenge if you take a break during your training, for example, to undertake research, go on a sabbatical or have children. Some doctors who have children and work part time can sacrifice their entire salary on childcare to return to work or complete their training. Furthermore, there are often contractual restrictions imposed on doctors who work part time that restrict them from taking on a second job. Having an alternative income stream to support you if your main income stream changes can be a lifesaver and allow us to enjoy financial stability and greater independence.

Doctors (like most people) can develop unhealthy spending habits

Unfortunately, some people develop unhealthy spending habits after qualifying. Check your bank statement to see where the majority of your wages go—is it the hospital coffee shop, take-away food, parking tickets or that gym membership you never get around to using? After years of being a student living on a shoestring budget while our non-medic friends happily progress in their careers (and salaries), some of us let go of the purse strings after qualifying. Excited about our new-found 'wealth' we go out spending on nice things, eat out more than we should, take part in the collective madness of payday parties, and buy all manner of material liabilities! Worse still, when it comes to settling down, marriage, having kids or even buying our first home it can be a rude awakening to find our lifestyle expectations are not met. It is easy to fall prey to consumer culture, the availability of easy credit and buying things we can't afford. In this way, people can quickly find themselves in thousands of pounds of unsecured debt.

If you're nodding your head and identify with this situation, you are not alone. Many of the doctors I have coached or mentored are in exactly this situation when they start out. Some time ago I coached an A&E consultant who was over £50,000 in debt. She was struggling to find a way out as she'd repeatedly made lifestyle choices that didn't match her salary. The cycle is hard to break when your day job consumes most of your time, energy and mindspace. It takes courage and honesty to assess the situation, make a plan, get out of debt, and eliminate damaging money habits. Unfortunately, most people haven't been taught about money management, investment or how to develop healthy financial habits. Investing in property brings with it a greater financial awareness which can positively impact your own spending habits.

Property investment can provide financial security

As doctors some of us may be relatively late starting work (mid-twenties or even later for those entering the profession as graduates). We can therefore be a few years behind in terms of earnings and pensions, depending on how our career pans out. The risk of doctors suffering burnout in the current healthcare system is high and we're at higher risk of mental health problems and suicide than many other professions. This means that some will retire earlier than expected. Female doctors, for example, are four times more likely to commit suicide than those in the general population. The Office for National Statistics recently reported that 430 healthcare professionals took their own lives in England between 2011-2015.[2] This is tragic and serves as a warning that we must take care of ourselves and

2 Dr Ben Windsor-Shellard, 'Suicide by Occupation, England 2011-2015, https://www.ons.gov.uk/peoplepopulationandcommunity/birthsdeathsandmarriages/deaths/articles/suicidebyoccupation/england2011to2015, (release date 17 March 2017), [accessed 11 November 2018].

one another. Creating financial stability plays a big part in this as financial worries are a common theme for people suffering from stress, anxiety and depression. While I would not wish ill health on anyone, it is prudent to consider how you might support yourself and your family if you were to fall sick. Would receiving benefits be enough to sustain your needs? An alternative income source can serve as a security blanket and give peace of mind to you and your family.

Moving on to those of you who have children. It's common sense that a shorter full-time working life (parents who take maternity leave included) can have an impact on overall earnings and final pensions.[3] In this regard it is useful to start thinking and planning for the future and for unexpected events. Ask yourself the following and jot down the answers:

1. How would you cope if you could no longer work as a doctor?
2. How long could you survive for without a regular salary?
3. Where would your income to cover living expenses come from?

Do your answers concern you? If so, it seems sensible to make a backup plan for alternative sources of income whether through property investment or not.

Property can serve as a good alternative to a pension

Will your pension conditions be upheld by the time you are sixty-eight? The NHS pension is currently one of the best available though many people find it incredibly difficult to obtain adequate information about their pension, let alone think that far ahead. While I'm not against paying into my NHS pension, it's unwise to rely completely on the state to provide for us. And it would be naïve to think our current pension terms will *definitely* be upheld by the

3 You can find out more about your NHS pension here: NHS Business Services Authority, NHS Pensions https://www.nhsbsa.nhs.uk/nhs-pensions [accessed 11 November 2018]

time we retire. With an increasing ageing population living longer than ever before, it may not be sustainable for the government to pay out thousands of pounds, to a load of elderly doctors living into their nineties (if burnout hasn't caught up with them, of course).

In any case, do you want to wait until you are sixty-eight to lead the life you want or to be truly financially independent? Even then, how long do you think you'll live for? Wouldn't you like the freedom to choose how to live your life prior to retirement? There has definitely been a change in attitude towards medical careers in recent years and most people long for greater autonomy, flexibility and work-life balance. The problem for most of us is that financially we cannot afford to reduce our working hours. In this regard, investing in property is a logical choice since you can supplement or replace your doctor's salary with rental income while the value of your property increases over time, providing you with a long-term valuable asset.

It is also possible to invest private pensions in property. The great thing about this is that with the right knowledge you can have more control and make better investment decisions (and gain far higher returns) than pension funds which invest on your behalf (and handsomely profit from your hard-earned cash over decades while giving you a minimal return). Don't get me wrong, some hands-free investments are great investments and much less work. Similarly, a good independent financial advisor (IFA) can be worth their weight in gold as they can advise you on how best to manage, save and invest your money. However, you may like the idea of being in control of your investments and being able to choose to 'retire' whenever you like as a result of creating alternative income streams.

Property allows you to enjoy your vocation!

Many of us start our careers feeling that medicine is a vocation, but over time the sense of passion and purpose that motivated us to become doctors diminishes as we get eaten up in the system and exhausted by the physical and emotional burden of the role. Life and reality take their toll and being a doctor quickly becomes a *job*, a means to an end, a way to survive and to pay the bills. Given the significant demands of a medical career, and the fact most people feel they have little control over their workload, working patterns, earning potential and the impact of the job on their personal lives, feelings of resentment and resignation can set in. No wonder complaints about poor bedside manner and lack of empathy are rife. It's never too late to turn things around and have a fantastic medical career by using property investment to give you more financial stability, choice and free time (no matter how old you are!).

Property has removed my need to work for survival. The small but profitable business I have grown has given myself (and my family) financial security and independence we would not be able to enjoy otherwise. At times I've received negative comments from some colleagues who, stuck in a negative mindset, say, *If you're so successful in property why would you EVER come back to work in the NHS?* I don't take offence at these remarks as people don't know what they don't know and usually project their negative beliefs about things they haven't experienced or don't understand. I believe in the values of the NHS. Being a doctor is a key part of who I am and it allows me to make a contribution to society. I also find it an immensely rewarding and stimulating career. Although the healthcare system is fraught with challenges, and staff are not looked after in the way they deserve, I still choose to go to work every day. The difference is I do it not because I have to, but because I want to.

Having had time out from medicine myself, I consider myself a more well-rounded person than before with a healthier perspective on my life and medical career. I developed skills and interests I didn't know I had and applied a whole lot of skills learned in medicine to property investment. My confidence grew and I started to feel positive and have fun again.

Ironically, not needing to work as a doctor to survive changed my mindset and has made me fall in love with my profession again—and it's re-kindled the curiosity for medicine and human psychology that attracted me to it in the first place! There are still things that annoy or upset me about the current system, but I can brush these off with greater ease as I have more control over my life. Medicine is one of the beautiful professions there is, and I hope to have a long and happy career alongside my other interests and help others to do the same.

Doctors are high rate tax payers and may need a back-up plan

No-one goes into medicine because they want to become rich but there are a number of assumptions made about doctors' earnings by the general public, and a great deal of ignorance within the profession about the way things work. I recently attended a training session on GP taxes and income and the vast majority of my colleagues were astounded (in some cases outraged) at how much they were going to be taxed on income from medical work, dividends from limited company earnings and other expenses related to running a medical business or working as a GP. As you may know, doctors are taxed 40% on income above £46,350 (as of 2018), and having to fund indemnity insurance, examinations, and numerous other expenses sometimes leaves little to play with at the end of the month. Even locum doctors are suffering with the introduction of the new IR35 rules[4] as they are no longer able to work for the NHS through an intermediary such as their own limited company. This means they pay much more tax and national insurance contributions than previously.

---

4 You can read about the IR35 rules that prohibit locum doctors providing services to the NHS through an intermediary such as a limited company, here: 'HM Revenue & Customs, Off-payroll working through an intermediary (IR35),' https://www.gov.uk/guidance/ir35-find-out-if-it-applies, (published 5 June 2014, updated 20 September 2017) [accessed 11 November 2018]

For some people, working as an employee in the current system doesn't make financial sense. Many GPs who work part time due to childcare commitments (but who could work a little more than part time) can't afford to work an extra half day per week due to the soaring medical indemnity insurance costs they would need to pay to cover their extra hours of clinical practice. They are in a lose-lose situation and so is our society. Unless working through a limited company (there are now few opportunities for this), doctors have to self-fund numerous professional expenses, only a fraction of which can be offset against tax.

If you can set yourself up to work through a limited company, there are numerous tax benefits which will allow you to protect more of your income by being able to offset your expenses, grow your company and make some investments too! Robert Kiyosaki's book *Rich Dad, Poor Dad* clearly explains this concept in simple terms and was one of the first books I read that inspired me to get into property. I strongly suggest that if you are a newly qualified GP looking to locum, you consult a specialist tax advisor on whether to work as an individual or through a limited company as it can have a huge impact on the way you're taxed. However, the point I'm making is that if you want to supplement your income as it is falling short of your expectations, property investment is a great way to do that.

Why property is a popular investment choice

Property is a great income generator

Investing in property is a great way to generate a side income (if you follow the rules and avoid making costly mistakes). For many people it provides a 'pension', cash lump sums or an entire business that contributes to the local economy. It also provides jobs for people and creates homes to live in. Property is an asset that can generate income for you in multiple ways. For example, rental income capital growth and income from equity release when you increase the value of the property through refurbishment or other value adds.

Property can give you your time back

Property can remove the need for you to work for survival. If you invest successfully, you could stop having to exchange your time for money and spend your time how, with whom, and wherever you like! Essentially, you can choose how to spend your time—a massive motivator for many people. What would you choose to do if you cut your work hours or took early retirement?

Property is a great way of leaving a legacy

Many people want to leave a legacy to their family, a charity, or even to society. Again, property allows you to do that, and when set up correctly it can be done in the most tax efficient and frictionless manner for those who will inherit your estate. It may be that property provides the funds to service that legacy or those premises! Would you like to leave a legacy to your family, friends or country one day?

Property can allow you to make different lifestyle choices

One property investor called Wendy Whittaker-Large who runs a business called 'Best Nest' started investing in property in order to leave a legacy to her children but quickly realised she also wanted to enjoy a certain lifestyle with them. To do this, she changed her strategy from single lets to *houses of multiple occupation* (HMOs) to benefit from the tremendous cash flow that HMOs generate. This gave her the freedom to enjoy a different lifestyle. Again, the income you can generate from property, and the fact that property allows you to work flexibly (remotely or from home), can be a massive draw for people who want to enjoy a certain lifestyle. This may be anything from travelling around the world running a business from your laptop to simply spending more time with your loved ones, indulging in new experiences or just being with the people you love when it matters the most! Investing in property (or any other asset) is not about getting rich or earning more money per se, it's about having more choice or freedom. If you want more choice or freedom, it's worth learning about how to best manage your money and consulting a good independent financial advisor (IFA) who can guide you on how to do this. The majority of property investors I know have IFAs to advise them on how to best invest the additional cash they earn from property, and for good reason.

Becoming a property investor is a great opportunity to become an entrepreneur!

This is one of the aspects I have most enjoyed. Property has allowed me to experience entrepreneurship, develop an entrepreneurial mindset, become a problem solver and job creator, exercise creativity and manage money far better than ever before. I love the thrill of chasing a good deal, building business relationships and collaborating with professionals in the industry from tradesmen to solicitors and architects to estate agents. I love the creativity within property, and I'm not just talking about interior design (which I get *really* excited about). Skills you soon develop as a property investor include thinking creatively about the way you structure deals, maximising the value in your property, finding funds, sourcing properties and much more. Running a property business allows you to develop skills and experience in areas such as accounting, people management, sales and marketing, project management, and business development. The process teaches you to think differently about both personal and professional matters, and I find myself applying an entrepreneurial mindset to most aspects of life now. Property can allow you to be your own boss and enjoy considerable independence. Property is also far easier a business to set up and run than any other business venture I've tried.

Property investing can be for everyone!

One of the things I most like about property is that compared to other asset classes it isn't difficult to understand or manage the risks involved. There will always be a risk to any investment you make, but in terms of predictability and having lots of options or contingency plans from the outset, property trumps it every time for me. Anyone can become a property investor if they want it enough and if they can follow the rules that will allow them to make wise choices and to manage risk. If you're a doctor, you are likely to be academically competent and have the potential to become an extremely successful property investor. All you need to do so is invest sometime in developing the knowledge and network you need to succeed, apply the transferable skills you developed in your medical career, and decide to get started. You owe it to yourself.

You don't need any prior experience to invest in property, so you can start from zero. Contrary to popular belief, you also don't need any money to start to invest in property. However, one thing some of you will struggle with is having enough time to focus a little on property. The good news is, there *are* ways to achieve your goals even if you don't have much time available. Where there's a will there's a way.

CHAPTER 2

SEVEN MYTHS THAT SHOULDN'T STOP YOU FROM INVESTING IN PROPERTY

There are a number of perceived challenges that stop people in their tracks when they first start thinking about investing in property. Unfortunately, for a lot of people I meet at my property courses and events, these challenges, as well as fear and a lack of relevant education, delay them getting started for many years. This includes me. If only I'd had the necessary knowledge and advice when I was in university. I could have started investing much earlier, quit the part time jobs I had, and taken advantage of other opportunities, instead. You don't know what you don't know, so if this story sounds familiar to you, don't beat yourself up about it. You're not alone. Forget the past, don't compare yourself to others and start from where you are without any regret or self-judgment. You can succeed and reading this book is a step in the right direction!

One of my favourite quotes is from Henry Ford who said, 'If you think you can, or you think you can't, then you're right'. Being successful in any area of your life is heavily influenced by mindset and the internal stories (or excuses) we play to ourselves over and over again.

I recently heard Jamil Qureshi (a performance psychologist who has trained some of the world's most successful athletes) speak at a novel property developers' club of which I'm a member. His talk was centred around how our thoughts translate to feelings which translate to actions and how the internal dialogue we continuously have with ourselves can hugely affect our performance. Thoughts—feelings—actions. The interesting thing is that whatever we spend the most time thinking about is what we end up moving towards. In other words, whatever you spend the most time focusing on is what grows. For example, those trying to get out of debt focusing on their debt rather than on the extra income they will make to pay off the debt. Many people's actions may be focused on moving away from negative situations or avoiding risk rather than considering the possibility of success or what would happen if they succeeded.

A great illustration of this was Jamil's story about a great footballer who was amazing when taking penalties. Every time this footballer took a penalty he asked himself the same question repeatedly while he ran up to kick the ball and only answered it just before kicking. *Will I run left or right after I score the penalty?* Scoring the goal was a given. He had already mentally primed himself into a positive, success mindset. His only question was which way he would run to celebrate his success—quite a different mindset to most people who may find themselves in that position, right?

Perhaps you've been watching the American TV series *Billions* which features a performance psychologist who works for an investment bank. Again, you may notice how the strategies she uses to hype the traders into a winning mindset state has a huge impact on their performance. The power of developing a success mindset cannot be overestimated.[5]

You may wonder how this relates to property. If you focus on factors you perceive as negative or risky and allow yourself to obsess over them, this could have a serious impact on your feelings and actions. The same goes for listening to negative people who don't know what they are talking about. A fear driven attitude will also affect how others perceive you and what sorts of opportunities come your way (or not). You shouldn't ignore risks or the facts of your personal situation. Instead, look at it differently by turning all possibilities and realities into statements, facts or questions, For example:

THOUGHT: *I have no funds to invest.*

FACT: *We need x funds for this project.*

QUESTION: *I wonder what funding sources are available for a project like this.*

5 You can listen to Jamil's talk on YouTube: Jamil Qureshi, Qandor Club, 'How to be No. 1', (uploaded 17 April 2018), https://www.youtube.com/watch?v=778ZizXgrgM [accessed 11 November 2018].

Similarly, when it comes to risk:

THOUGHT: *The property market is too risky at the moment.*

FACT: *There are risks I should be aware of in the property market at the moment.*

QUESTION: *What exit strategies/plans can I come up with to mitigate the risks or if things don't go to plan?*

It is useful to mentally check-in with yourself like this to ensure you are as objective as possible and don't give up before you even get started. Don't forget that as medics we are generally capable at managing risk and most of our perceptions of risk outside of medicine are largely associated with a fear of the unknown.

I don't have enough money

By far, the most common reason that you may think you can't invest in property is the assumption you need *some*, if not *a lot*, of money to buy your first property. I thought exactly the same before I learned more about property investment! This is a linear way of thinking and unfortunately no one has taught us to think about investment creatively. This assumption is not true for three reasons:

1. It assumes that the only way to invest in a property is to buy one in the conventional way.
2. It assumes that investing in a property must be with your own money.
3. It assumes that you need a lot of money to get started.

The good news is that none of the above are true! If they were, how on earth do you think professional property investors keep their businesses going? How do you think any business ever gets going? Entrepreneurs and start-ups frequently have to raise funding for their businesses and property fundraising is similar. Furthermore, don't let a lack of experience in doing this put you off. In July 2018, I had the pleasure of hosting the NHS Clinical Entrepreneur programme's end of year event called 'The Big Pitch' at Bloomberg HQ in London, where we celebrated the achievements of the entrepreneurs, one of which was that over £113 million pounds of funding has been raised in the first two years.[6] Yes, by doctors. No, not out of their own pockets! At some point, everyone will run out of funds once they have finished purchasing properties, buildings or land sites and they have to learn to look at alternative funding sources. If you have a good enough business proposition, you'll find the money required to support it.

TOP TIP

Develop a money mindset of abundance. Money is simply a resource that can be accessed in a variety of ways once you know how. Being open minded and positive, helping people without expecting anything in return, and always being honest and ethical in business will result in people, funding and opportunities coming your way.

I don't have any experience

The issue of not having enough experience to get into property or assuming you need to be a 'professional' investor is common. Perhaps even more so within the medical profession as we are accustomed to studying hard for formal qualifications and providing evidence that we are adequately skilled to do something. Developing knowledge and expertise will always be valuable in any field. However, you **do not need any prior experience or qualifications to become a property investor!** No offence to any investors out there, but compared to medicine, property investing is pretty straightforward, and you can become a successful property investor in a fraction of

6 The NHS Clinical Entrepreneur Programme is a twelve month programme designed to offer opportunities for junior doctors and wider health professionals to develop their entrepreneurial aspirations during their clinical training period. You can find out more about how to apply here: Clinical Entrepreneur Training Programme, NHS England, https://www.england.nhs.uk/ourwork/innovation/clinical-entrepreneur/ [accessed 11 November 2018].

the time it takes to become a doctor! Experience is always beneficial, but it's not a prerequisite. All you need to do is make sure you invest some time in developing your property knowledge and skills and build a supportive network of people who can help you if you get stuck. In this regard, it is no different to being a doctor in training or a clinical entrepreneur developing clinical skills and expertise over time. It just happens a bit faster in property-land.

You may also be apprehensive about becoming a property owner or landlord and the responsibility that comes with that. It's a legitimate concern and I'm going to show you exactly how to best prepare for that, how to become a professional landlord within twenty-four hours, and the common mistakes and pitfalls to avoid. Furthermore, in stark contrast to the crazy hours, risk, stress and sheer terror you may have experienced as a house officer, this is a walk in the park. Like a Spartan warrior, you have been trained and have the skills you need to succeed.

TOP TIP

Don't let your lack of experience or knowledge put you off—like when you prepare for an exam, you can only start from where you are. Once you decide you really want to get into property investment the most important thing is to get started as soon as possible. Like now. What are you waiting for?

I don't have any time

This is another common reason (or excuse) when it comes to explaining why you can't invest right now. We all have the same twenty-four hours in a day so why do some people manage to achieve more within the same time period? Some of the busiest people I know have achieved incredible things, and yet they're seemingly people who are short of time. As the saying goes, if you want to get something done, give it to a busy person. So how do you do more when resources such as time are finite? This is down to the power of leverage. Doctors are busy people, and when it comes to shift work and the nature of the job itself, it can feel like there is little time or fuel in the tank to do anything other than collapse in front of Netflix at the end of the day. One way to get around this, if you are *really* short of time, is to leverage other people's time and expertise to help you to achieve your mutual goals. All you need to do is decide why you want to invest in property, what your goals are, how you will achieve them, and who you need to help (as well as motivate) you along the way. This might mean using a property sourcer to help you find great deals, setting up searches on property portals, using a lettings agent to manage your properties, or doing a joint venture with someone else who has more time than you and can do the majority of the leg work!

When people hear that I am in full time training they ask, 'How do you do it?' The truth is that I have learnt to be ruthless with my time and realistic about what I can achieve, and I've chosen to work with great partners which allows me to keep moving forward. I don't always get it right with time management but I'm always continually improving. One of the reasons it has taken me so long to write this book is because of balancing multiple projects—something had to give. Burnout is common not only in medicine but in the entrepreneur field too, and I want to avoid that at all costs. Instead, I'm happy to go slower and enjoy the journey!

You don't have to do it on your own, either. In fact, you can't do it alone. In your average property transaction you're likely to need an accountant, solicitor, mortgage broker, builder, estate or lettings agent, handyman, tenant referencing service and more! You'll achieve far more, and faster by working with others, allowing them to help you and helping them out when you can in return. There are a number of ingenious ways to get help through employing virtual assistants (VAs) as well as a number of other professionals who can do your admin and any 'low value' activities that consume a lot of time, hence giving you your personal time back!

TOP TIP

If you're short of time, think about how you can leverage other people's time to achieve your goals. If you want to go it alone, bear in mind that you may need to pay for someone else's time to do tasks you don't have time for. If you're considering a joint venture with someone, think about whether you are able to bring knowledge, experience, special skills, funds or any other valuable asset into the partnership in exchange for your partner's time.

Property investing is too risky

I love this one. There is certainly a great deal of anxiety around taking on a large debt, such as a mortgage, but this anxiety might be alleviated if you understand the difference between good debt and bad debt. There is a risk to property investing, but honestly, what *isn't* risky? There is a risk to crossing the road. We take on risks every day we go to work, assess patients, write prescriptions and write up medical notes. Yes, there is a risk to property investment, but you can educate yourself to understand what that risk is (specific to your strategy) and take measures that allow you to mitigate it as far as possible. For example, always have a contingency plan (ideally, three exit strategy options in case things don't go to plan) and follow some simple investment rules that will safeguard you against making terrible mistakes in the first place. The fear of risk seems to stem mainly from a lack of knowledge and understanding about how property investment and the market cycle works. How can you form an opinion a subject if you have little or no knowledge about it?

Contrast the fear of risk in property to the risks we take every day in the profession. There is a great deal of risk involved for the patients we treat as they trust us to treat them or guide them in life or death decisions. We are continually treating acute and life-threatening conditions or trying our best to prevent them from occurring. While at work we dodge sharps injuries, work for hours on end without adequate fluids or rest (hands up who has had a UTI after a week of on-calls!), and work night upon night with the health risks we know will result from turning our diurnal rhythm upside down, yet onwards we plough.

We also risk our mental health from the responsibility we take on and the stresses, strains and number of emotionally intense situations we experience along the way. Naturally, at some point in our careers our social lives and personal relationships are affected—God forbid that your other half is a doctor!

As doctors we risk *a lot*! What's the worst that can happen?

The death or serious injury of a patient or even yourself. Pretty serious stuff. Compare this to the financial risks involved in property. For example, you lose your money, you lose a property through defaulting on payments, you get a bad credit record, or (worst-case scenario) you become homeless. This can be mitigated in the first place but, if it does happen, it's far easier to bounce back from something like that than the various disasters related to working in medicine or being investigated by the General Medical Council as a result of a complaint about your clinical practice.

There are many different types of investment. Some investors have an appetite for high risk (and high reward) ventures and others prefer to stick to medium or low risk ventures (with commensurate low to medium reward). There is no right or wrong as long as you know what the worst thing that could happen is and feel comfortable with taking that risk.

TOP TIP

There is always a risk to investing; do thorough due diligence, be conservative, and make contingency plans for worst case scenarios.

The market isn't right

This is one phrase I've heard used by many amateur investors of late and with the newspapers reporting the doom and gloom of recession, Brexit, a hung parliament and recent property tax changes, who can blame them?

The problem with taking advice from the newspaper or your next-door neighbour is that by the time the news has filtered down to the masses, it's usually time to do the opposite of what is being reported. As Warren Buffet says, 'Be fearful when others are greedy and greedy when others are fearful.'

There are two factors here you must be aware of. Firstly, the property market is cyclical which means it will always move through boom and bust phases. Secondly, there are different investment strategies that can be used in different phases of the market cycle (it's not all about buying and selling to produce a profitable investment). One example is the retirement living sector. This is a billion-pound industry that plenty of companies (as well as investment funds) are moving into. Are they scared off by the state of the current market, Brexit etc. In short, no. Why?

Successful property investors and developers take a long-term view and consider long-term demographic and societal trends. Therefore, provided you understand the property market cycle and know which part of the cycle you are in, you should be able to invest successfully regardless of what the market is doing. Simple right?

TOP TIP

Make sure you understand which part of the market cycle you are in and whether the strategy you're using will work in that phase of the cycle.

I'm too old (or too young!) to start

This one makes me smile as I truly believe you are never too old to start anything. My parents are a constant source of inspiration to me as they endeavour to learn new things, develop new hobbies, and take on new challenges over time. With people living well into their nineties and even over a hundred, why not! There are some investors within my network who have started out in their fifties and sixties (and yes, they can still obtain mortgages). Listen up: it's never too late! For a dose of inspiration read about the tremendous achievements of medical student Will Gao at the end of this chapter.

TOP TIP

Age is not relevant to property investment. If you start networking, you will soon meet someone the same age as you or many years older. Property investing is for everyone.

The tax rules have changed: it's not worth it any more

Don't believe everything you read in the papers! Yes, the tax rules have changed. Yes, we are currently in a downward part of the property market cycle with ongoing uncertainty about how Brexit and other factors will affect it. Does this mean property is no longer a profitable asset class? Of course it doesn't. Rules change, so you have to learn to be flexible and adapt. Investors who once purchased in their own names are now incorporating. Investors whose main strategy was flipping (buying to sell) properties for a profit may now be buying houses of multiple occupation and flipping only when the right opportunity comes along or when the market picks up.

One financial advisor at an event I attended told an audience of doctors he wouldn't touch BTL with a barge-pole and they would be better off getting a 5-7% return investing in stocks, shares and other financial products. I was perturbed by this as it gave a one-sided view and I approached him in the break to find out why he had made such a blanket statement. He told me that he said this due to the recent Section 24 tax changes affecting people who invest in their personal names (we discuss these tax changes in more detail in Chapter 3). When pressed further, he acknowledged that great profits can be made from property when you know how (most people don't). The bottom line is that people have their own agendas and will only tell you the story they want you to hear. It's important to understand the full picture by educating yourself and be able form your own opinion.

Naturally, property is not the only asset to invest in, but given my lack of knowledge about stocks and shares or trading, property is currently lower risk and more accessible to me. It is definitely higher reward than investing in most ISAs (for a 3% return, for example) and much, much better than leaving your money to depreciate in the bank as inflation slowly erodes its value over time. The inflation rate at the time of writing this book is 2.2%[7] which means any money you have in the bank, needs to be earning 2.2% interest to remain at the same value. You can make far, far more than 2.2% return per year by investing in property all over the UK and further afield. Personally, I love the fact that property is an asset you can easily understand and control and, as one doctor says, you can 'scratch and sniff' it. You can also make some incredible contacts, provide people in your community with a comfortable home, build a sustainable business and apply your business skills to healthcare, too!

TOP TIP

Successful investors learn to be flexible and adapt to changes in the market place by using strategies that are appropriate at that time.

7 Andy King, UK Office for National Statistics, April 2018, 'Consumer Price Inflation, UK: September 2018', https://www.ons.gov.uk/economy/inflationandpriceindices/bulletins/consumerpriceinflation/september2018 (published 17 October 2018), [accessed 11 November 2018].

CASE STUDY

William Gao: medical student, University College, London

After a series of unexpected turns in life, I found myself completely out of my depth in the world of property. One year later, I'm delighted to say that, with invaluable guidance from Lafina, I've achieved what I thought previously was impossible. Firstly, my brother and I have completed our first ever deal for a flat in south London and, secondly, I have helped my dad, who has worked as a chef his entire life, to complete a restaurant-to-flat conversion on our old family house/restaurant to give him his well-deserved early retirement.

As bizarre and foreign as property may have seemed to me at first, funnily, it draws many parallels to my experiences of the world of clinical medicine. As a fresh-faced student of both of these fascinating fields, I suffered many setbacks in the beginning and decided to immerse myself in all things property related—ranging from books to podcasts all the way to networking events. But the most pivotal support I received was from Lafina, because being a newbie with only a basic grasp of the concepts of property, I constantly found myself in pits of analysis paralysis and couldn't bring myself to take decisive action. Having a mentor to support me on those occasions gave me the much-needed confidence to follow through with the deals.

My journey has certainly not been without its pitfalls. Last autumn we eventually had our first ever offer accepted on a flat in the heart of Croydon that was selling below the market value—ideal, right? I sourced a local solicitor and naively thought the job was done. However, a couple of months later problems on the seller's side (worsened by my solicitor dodging calls and going on holiday with no colleague to cover) meant that the deal fell through. We were devastated. First brutal lesson learned—find a reliable solicitor.

Bouncing back from this tragic defeat with renewed enthusiasm in 2018, we eventually sourced another flat in the heart of Croydon. We again had an offer accepted and this time we ensured the sellers weren't likely to pull out—and yes, we did find a new solicitor. Wiser from our prior experience, we did everything we could to ensure this one didn't fall through, using advanced negotiation techniques right up until the exchange of contracts.

I'm pleased to say, we're now fully moved in.

Moving out of our family house opened up the pathway for my dad to convert our old family home (which was split downstairs as an old restaurant and upstairs as our living quarters) into individual flat units to rent out. This project was met with a whole new set of challenges. My biggest surprise was discovering how much variation there was between builders' quotations for the same job. I opted to play it safe and commissioned an old school friend of mine in the plumbing trade to do the job for us. After months of work, we're due to rent out the flats to tenants through a lettings agency.

Property has had a profound impact on my and my family's lives. It has been thoroughly enjoyable (now I look back on it) and I am beginning to feel the benefits of our labour. I am most proud to say my dad is currently planning his once-in-a-lifetime trip around the world from London back to his hometown (Shanghai, China). This would not have been made possible without property and at last, for once, he's not working for his money; his money is working for him.

Projects:

1 bedroom flat, East Croydon; 125-year leasehold 55m^2, £275,000 (£215,000 via a 35-year mortgage with Halifax fixed at 2% for five years with a £60,000 borrowed up front deposit.

House to three flat conversion, Carshalton, Surrey

Refurb costs:

£2,700 plumbing (new combination boiler fitted with dual-valves, so residents have personal control)

£3,000 for electricians (separate 3x fuse meters)

£2,000 for plastering all walls (four rooms in total)
£1,700 for new floorboards and labour
£2,000 for two kitchens
£1,600 for white goods (two fridge freezers and two washing machines)
£1,800 for complete decoration, painting and snagging loose ends

Total: Around £15,000.

My dad will live in one of the apartments. The other two rent for ~£1,000 pcm each, giving my dad a retirement income of £24,000 per annum from the rental profits.

CHAPTER 3

THE CURRENT UK PROPERTY MARKET AND FACTORS THAT INFLUENCE IT

Understanding the property market cycle, coupled with having adequate knowledge of different investment strategies, is essential if you are to invest successfully. Just like decision making and clinical management of patients in medicine, you need to be able to assess risk and select a management strategy while accounting for the worst case scenario or complications that can occur. The multitude of factors that affect the housing market can be complex so (while you don't have to become an economist overnight) the more you try to learn and understand about the housing market, the better.

Just like in general practice where you cannot be an expert in every single medical speciality, it's the same with property investment. From time to time you will need to seek expert advice. (the land of the expert generalist), you can't be an expert in everything property related. If you try to do everything yourself or think you know it all, you'll get caught out at some point. The key is knowing how to safely manage risk and where to find the expert advice you require when you need it. I'm constantly learning new things about property, and as the market changes or new legislation is introduced, I always try to learn as much as I can from an expert in that field. For example, when new legislation affecting property income was introduced recently, I read over the basics myself, then had a discussion with my accountant about how this would affect me and what changes I would need to make to my strategy in the future. There was no one better qualified than my accountant to advise me on this. Before I decide to sell a property, I'll have an in-depth discussion with one of my trusted estate agent contacts. Not because I can't hop onto Rightmove.com and take a look at property prices myself (I do this, anyway), but because estate agents are selling property day in day out and know how much stock they are actually shifting, how many buyers there are, what the market demand is like, and the sales prices that are being agreed in reality.

Property market cycle: the basics

Supply and demand

The simplest way to understand the market for any product is to look at supply and demand. Ask yourself whether there's a demand for the product you are selling (and whether there are there customers/buyers) and assess the supply of the product (is there enough stock)? In general, house prices or rents may be driven up when there is high demand or low supply. Conversely, when demand for a product drops or there is over-supply, the cost of the product drops. In the housing market, house prices and rents fall if the market is too saturated with stock or if people stop buying.

Boom and bust

You can also think of the market in terms of boom and bust. House prices rise in response to increased demand and fall when there isn't enough demand. When prices are rising rapidly and reaching the peak of the market cycle, this is the *boom* phase. When prices start falling, the market is described as *correcting* or heading for recession and when prices reach the bottom, this is known as the *bust* phase of the market. Just like with stocks and shares, investors want to buy property when prices are low (for example, during a recession) and sell when demand drives prices up high again (for example, during a rising or boom market). However, you don't need to wait for a recession to find a cheap property to buy. It's possible to buy properties below market value (BMV) in any market.

The interesting thing about the value of property is that (despite this boom-bust cycle) the value of property over many decades steadily increases. This is thanks to inflation (as the cost of living rises, so do salaries, rents and property values), as well as the general difficulty that the country has had in reaching government targets for housebuilding and the general shortage of homes. Look at any data on property values over the last hundred years and you will see the general trend is upwards. If you invest using specific rules and criteria (and take a long-term approach), you're likely to live through one or two market cycles and enjoy profitable investments. This doesn't mean you should rely on inflation to make a profit or that investment is not at risk during these periods. There are many reasons for investments going wrong such as greed or recklessness, inadequate knowledge, over-stretching yourself financially or taking unnecessary risks.

What's the relevance of the property market cycle?

Different strategies for different parts of the cycle

At the time of publishing (late 2018) we are in a downward phase of the property market cycle. Some people will preach doom and gloom while others see opportunity. The latter are usually seasoned investors playing the long game in property and who know now is the time to buy properties cheaply or use specific strategies that work in this part of the cycle. There are always exceptions to the rule and many strategies can be used at *any time* if the criteria are right at *entry and exit*. For example, it's not impossible to flip a property in a falling market if you buy cheap and sell at the right price but it may well be much harder and less profitable. Below are some of the strategies most commonly used during rising and following markets.

Rising market

Buy-to-let

Buy-to-flip

Buy-refurbish-refinance (to release capital)

Developments and build to sell schemes.

Falling market

Rent-to-rent

Multi-lets

Lease options

Serviced accommodation

Build-to-rent

Social housing and care homes

During a rising or booming market you can buy to sell for a profit (flipping) even if buying at full market value, as the value of the property rapidly increases. In a falling market, this is a risky strategy as you may get caught out and suffer a significant drop in the value of your property, meaning you would either be forced to hold it or sell at a loss. However, knowledge is power as they say, and some of the most useful skills you can learn as a property investor are how to:

1. Appraise a deal
2. De-risk a deal using different exit strategies
3. Think flexibly and adapt your strategy to market changes

For example, take the above example of flipping a property when the market is in recession or about to crash. To de-risk a deal like this you should always try to buy a property below market value (as you will automatically be locking in profit from Day 1) and allow yourself a buffer in the event that the market changes and prices fall. Ideally, you should aim to have three exit strategies. For example, if you buy to flip and find you can't flip and need your cash back, you should be prepared to:

1. Hold and rent it out (ensuring the market rent more than covers any mortgage interest payable)
2. Sell and break even in the event you need cash back
3. Try to refinance cash back out if the property value has increased due to the market or changes you've made
4. Offer an investor a good rate of interest in return for a loan (if possible, secured against the property)

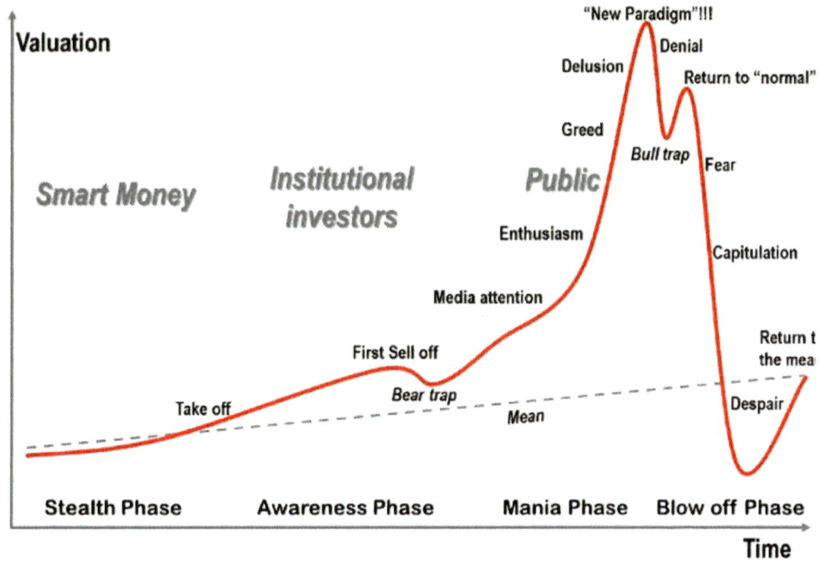

There are many illustrations of the property market cycle available online. This one, provided by Dr Jean-Paul Rodrigue at Hofstra University, New York[8] is by far the most descriptive I have come across in terms of different market cycle stages and the buying behaviour within each stage. Interestingly, it can be applied to a multitude of assets.

What factors affect supply and demand?

There is a myriad of micro and macroeconomic factors that affect the property market by impacting supply and demand. I'm not an expert in economics but I can give you examples of legislation and taxes affecting the UK housing market recently. The most obvious are the changes to stamp duty on second homes, the wear and tear allowance, and Section 24. The political environment also has an impact, for example, Brexit and the hung parliament.

Legislation and tax changes

8 Dr Jean-Paul Rodrigue, 'The Stages in a Bubble', https://transportgeography.org/?page_id=9035 (2017), [accessed 11 November 2018].

Stamp Duty Land Tax (SDLT) on second homes and removal of the wear and tear allowance

SDLT is a tax payable to HMRC when you purchase a property. The amount you pay depends on the price of the property and the price bracket this falls into. SDLT rates used to be the same for both residential and investment properties, regardless of how many properties you owned, but in 2015 the government changed the rules and added a 3% SDLT surcharge to second homes or second investment property purchases from April 2016 (i.e. someone who is looking to buy a buy to let [BTL] but does not own their home will not pay the surcharge).

The stamp duty rates for second purchases are set out below.

Buy-to-let and second home Stamp Duty tax bands[9]

Brackets	Standard rate	Buy-to-let/second home rate (1st April 2016)
Up to £125,000	0%	3%
£125,001 - £250,000	2%	5%
£250,001 - £925,000	5%	8%
£925,001 - £1.5m	10%	13%
over £1.5m	12%	15%

9 More information on SDLT rates can be found here: 'Stamp Duty Land Tax', *HM Revenue & Customs* https://www.gov.uk/stamp-duty-land-tax/residential-property-rates [accessed 11 November 2018].

First-time buyer SDLT relief

First-time buyers (FTBs) buying their first home in England, Wales and Northern Ireland (intended for personal use only) will not pay stamp duty up to £300,000 . For purchases over this amount, they will pay the standard rate for the excess over £300,000.[10] FTBs can't get SDLT relief on BTL/investment properties as you must be purchasing a property you intend to live in. Being classified as a first-time buyer is about home ownership, so if you have ever owned or inherited a residential property or are named on the deeds for your parents' home or any other home, you're not considered to be a first-time buyer and won't be eligible for SDLT relief.

Buying an investment property as a FTB

If you're a first-time buyer buying a BTL or investment property bear in mind you will:

1. Pay SDLT at the lower rate on if it is your first purchase.
2. Lose the FTB stamp duty relief if your residential purchase is your second purchase.
3. Not be eligible for the FTB Help-to-Buy scheme (FTB' can buy a residential property with just a 5% deposit and a government equity loan plus mortgage).[11]

Don't get too worried about having to pay extra stamp duty for second homes or investment properties. It's great to get SDLT relief and save thousands of pounds, but if you consider that capital appreciation in most areas will be 3-5% upwards per year, paying a little extra SDLT at the outset is not so significant in the long term (albeit annoying as it is another upfront expense to pay and factor

10 Find out more about the FTB SDLT allowance at: 'Stamp Duty Land Tax: relief for first time buyers', HM Revenue & Customs https://www.gov.uk/government/publications/stamp-duty-land-tax-relief-for-first-time-buyers (22 November 2017), [accessed 11 November 2018].

11 More info on the help to buy scheme can be found at:, 'Help to Buy', HM Government https://www.helptobuy.gov.uk [accessed 11 November 2018].

into your budget). Also, remember that you should be making your profits when you buy (by buying cheap or adding value in some way) and not relying exclusively on capital appreciation!

Wear and tear allowance

The wear and tear allowance was a special tax benefit for landlords which provided an automatic tax relief on 10% of the annual rental income. This was meant to reflect wear and tear on items in a furnished rental property. This benefit has now been scrapped, though any items being repaired or replaced due to damage can still be offset against tax.

Both wear and tear and SDLT changes impacted the market in a few ways. They caused a knee-jerk temporary surge in house sales in the months prior to the new second home SDLT rates being enforced. People rushed to purchase before the law was enforced which would cost them thousands extra in SDLT. Over the longer term, it decreased demand in parts of the market where the increase in stamp duty took a huge chunk of profit out of 'deals', rendering them unattractive to investors (for example, properties over £500,000). It also put off a lot of amateur investors from buying a second home or BTL, due to increased upfront expenses. From a lending perspective, FTB mortgage applications have increased and BTL mortgages have decreased due to the various FTB initiatives in an otherwise uncertain marketplace.

Section 24

This piece of legislation introduced in April 2017 (to take full effect by 2020/21) means you'll no longer be able to offset 100% of your mortgage interest expenses against tax on rental income. This is regardless of the fact that 30-50% of the income might be spent on paying mortgage interest.

In other words, mortgage interest is no longer considered a valid expense for landlords who have purchased investment properties in their own name. They will be taxed on the gross rental income rather than their net profits. Section 24 is currently being phased in to allow people to plan ahead, but by 2020/21, you will only be able to offset 20% of your mortgage interest expenses against tax.

Let's look at an example to understand how this could affect you. Imagine you earn £20,000 a year in rental income from one property but your mortgage costs you £15,000. Under the old system you would have been taxed on the £5,000 of actual profit made (mortgage interest was previously considered a 100% tax allowable expense). Due to Section 24, if you have purchased a property in your own name, you will now be paying tax on almost all the £20,000 of rental income with a small tax relief of 20% for finance costs. Other expenses such as repairs, professional fees and advertising will still be offset against tax. See a simple example below:

Rental income £20,000

Mortgage £15,000 (20% of £15,000 = £3,000 and only this amount can be offset against tax)

Actual rental profits £5,000

Total taxable rental income £17,000 at your personal income tax rate

Tax payable at 20% rate = £3,400

Tax payable at 40% rate = £6,800

The example above illustrates how the 40% tax payer will end up paying more than they have earned, hence incurring debt.

This new tax rule has been particularly painful for 40% tax payers and BTL landlords with large portfolios. It means that 40% taxpayers will pay even more tax on rental income, and those whose tax liability exceeds the net profits made will be pushed into debt (on their property). It also means that 20% taxpayers may become 40% taxpayers overnight if their gross rental income plus income from other sources (for example, NHS salary) takes them into the higher rate tax payer bracket.

The impact of these changes has been that:

1. Some amateur and small business investors have dropped out of the market.

2. Some small developers have left the residential market, turning to the commercial property market instead (which has some interesting tax benefits).

3. Landlords and investors with encumbered (mortgaged) BTL portfolios rendered unprofitable by the changes may sell poor performing stock and pay down some of their mortgages. They might also decide they have had enough and sell up altogether.

4. Some investors will decide to incorporate their property portfolio and switch existing mortgages to limited company mortgage products. This is because any property purchased within a company structure will be exempt from Section 24, meaning that mortgage interest can be offset against tax.

Political environment and impact on the property market

Brexit and the hung parliament

You may have noticed that the UK housing market has been significantly affected by politics over the last year or so. Factors such as the hung parliament and rows over Brexit have caused a period of instability and loss of confidence in the market. Experts are still postulating about the knock-on effect this will have on every industry, including the property market. Only recently, newspapers reported that house prices are expected to drop 30-40% in the event of a no-deal Brexit. Despite the UK being a pretty stable country, these events have caused much uncertainty and speculation in what has generally been a strong market over the past five years. When reports of doom and gloom in the property market dominate the headlines, it naturally influences buying and selling behaviour, which in turn affects the market.

However, a weak pound and property market crash will also attract investors looking for opportunities. In fact, many UK investors are going on a buying spree as prices fall. The problem in a falling market is that no one quite knows exactly when the market will bottom out and start to rise again. Therefore, rather than waiting for the bottom, sometimes it's best to grab a bargain when you can! Opportunism aside, market volatility may or may not be relevant to you depending on what you're buying, why you're buying it and how you're funding the purchase. For example, if you're buying your own home with a low interest rate repayment mortgage and can pretty much guarantee you'll be in employment for the foreseeable future, market crashes and recessions are unlikely to affect you. The same goes for long-term investment purchases. You need to protect yourself as far as possible from big jumps in interest rates (for example, by not having > 50-60% mortgages on your property or by fixing the interest you will pay for a certain period of time).

Cost of finance

Mortgage interest rates and the appetite of banks to lend also affect the property market. Interest rates have been unbelievably low for the last decade with the bank of England (BoE) base rate only rising from 0.5% to 0.75% in August 2018. As a result, the cost of borrowing has been extremely affordable and has allowed many people to get on the housing ladder and make fantastic profits from property (albeit without much skill involved) since the last recession in 2007. Contrast this with the late nineties when bank interest rates were at catastrophic levels of 18%—it's hard to believe but is a good reminder that we need to stress test our deals to understand at which point they'll start to fail and what our contingency plan would be. Bear in mind that small rises in interest rates needn't be feared as usually they'll be in line with inflation and rent rises.

In addition to interest rates, mortgage lending criteria also affect the market. If banks make their lending criteria stricter or mortgages less affordable, fewer people will be able to access finance, which naturally affects investment behaviour and general demand.

CASE STUDY

Dr Stephanie Bright, GP and property investor

One of my coaching clients recently spent some time considering this dilemma. Her initial priority and concerns were around waiting for the markets to fall low enough for her to get a bargain property and not buy a property without it decreasing in value afterwards.

This is a valid concern and one shared by many, but I reminded her that being in negative equity (when your house is worth less than what you purchased it for) would only be a problem if she needed to sell or flip the property in the next few years, which would put her at risk of selling at a loss. Since she was investing for the long-term and had some money saved up in the bank (de-valuing at a rate of 2.2% per annum thanks to inflation!) she reached the conclusion that rather than waiting for years for the market to bottom out, it would be more worthwhile to purchase a property with high cash flow or find a property that was being sold below market value to get her money working hard for her ASAP!

We found some properties in the north of England that would allow her to receive a projected return on investment of 27% on her cash deposit and the rental yield would be 17% (yes, it was a multi-let property!). Comparing this to leaving her money sitting in the bank and eroding over time, it was a total no-brainer!

Why is the UK property market a good place to invest?

The UK has always been a popular place to live, attracting people from all over the world who come to study, work, live and invest. Accommodation is in short supply and with an ever-increasing population, the demand for housing is higher than ever. In fact, we're in the midst of a housing shortage crisis. The UK is a stable place to live with high standards of living, so naturally people want to live here and will continue to do so. London alone requires 66,000 new homes per year to keep up with population growth and demand and we are currently only managing to build around 30,000 homes a year.[12] In the UK we need to be building 300,000 new homes a year to meet demand and we currently build around 200,000. For the next few decades at least, it seems that UK property will continue to be a strong asset to invest in. However, nothing is guaranteed and you should always stay abreast of trends and market changes.

TOP TIPS

Study the property market cycle, understand which part of the cycle you are in and what strategies are working in your area. Develop criteria that will safeguard you against suboptimal market conditions and over-exposure, and network with other investors to learn from their mistakes and successes.

Understand the factors driving demand and supply in your market and in particular how it affects your strategy.

Always take tax planning and financial advice before investing in property.

Stress-test your investment and think of contingency plans if market conditions are suboptimal.

Learn about different strategies so you can evaluate the best way to maximise the value of your asset.

Stay up to date with the market cycle by reading reports from organisations such as Savills.co.uk, Hometrack.com, and Propertyweek.com.

12 Full article available here: 'Mayor of London London Assembly, London 'needs 66,000 homes a year', https://www.london.gov.uk/city-hall-blog/london-needs-66000-new-homes-year, (27 October 2017), [accessed 11 November 2018].

CHAPTER 4

KEY CONCEPTS IN PROPERTY INVESTMENT YOU MUST UNDERSTAND

When you're searching for a property to invest in, how do you know whether it's a good deal? Are there any rules to follow that guide you in what makes a property 'investable' or not? Unfortunately, most doctors I meet have no idea where to start; they don't know how to appraise a deal and have no clear investment criteria. Their investment decisions are often based on factors such as what they can afford to buy, the aesthetics of a property, or what family and friends think. In the worst cases, the trusting doctor might fall prey to the persuasive powers of sales agents. It's like trying to practise medicine without using any evidence-based guidance! This can lead to a lot of trouble later down the line if you invest without any strategy whatsoever, without applying investment criteria and without considering what the market is doing.

On the courses we run at Eurekadoc we ensure you have a good understanding of property investment terminologies, as well as the basic concepts of investment. This allows you to formulate your own specific investment criteria so you can make investment decisions that suit your circumstances. One of our delegates, a GP from Birmingham, was thrilled to learn these concepts and be able to apply strict criteria to her search right away. Until that point, she'd been assessing properties based on the asking price and whether she liked the decor or not. It can feel like a minefield out there if you don't know how to calculate whether a deal makes sense or not!

Assets and liabilities

Do you consider buying your home an asset or a liability? If you think it's an asset, you are not alone—the vast majority of people are of the same opinion. I was too, until I read Robert Kiyosaki's *Rich Dad, Poor Dad*, which influenced the way I think about investment and money management. In certain circumstances your home may turn out to be a great asset. For example, if you buy a property to live in during a rising market and its value increases, you can benefit from the tax-free profits generated, if and when it's sold, or you can release some equity. This is not always the case, and if the value of your property is lower than the price you paid at the time you need to sell, it will have become a liability. However, the main reasons some people consider buying a home a liability are:

1. It generates no income while you live in it (unless you take on a lodger; a good strategy if you need extra cash and don't mind sharing your home since you can benefit from £7,500 in tax free rental income).
2. You can't offset the expense of mortgage interest against income tax.

As people advance in their careers, get promoted and get paid a higher salary, it's common for their spending to increase. Although there may be a big income gap and difference in lifestyle between someone earning £20,000 and £100,000 a year, often both earners are financially in the same situation, with no assets and lots of liabilities. If you're employed by a large organisation and want to get paid more, you usually need to work harder and longer hours. Unfortunately, the pay increase is often not worth the effort due to increased tax liability. A lot of doctors working gruelling hours are simply not interested in working locum or bank shifts on a regular basis as the financial reward isn't high enough to justify the sacrifice of using their free time to do more shift work.

Buying your own home is an emotional purchase, and you may have completely different criteria when buying it compared to buying an investment property. That's fine as it's a personal matter, but understanding the key principles of investment will help you make educated decisions and hopefully prevent you from making costly mistakes.

Equity and debt

Most people buy a property using a mortgage. They will do this using a cash deposit (often from their savings) and borrow the rest from the bank to be able to make the purchase. The cash amount forming the deposit is referred to as *equity* and the cash coming from the bank mortgage/loan as *debt*. There is good and bad debt. Good debt can be considered as any debt that forms part of an investment that will generate income or grow in value. It's also usually low-interest (for example, student loans or residential mortgages). Bad debt is debt incurred to purchase things that don't generate income or that decrease in value. It's usually high interest debt and is much riskier as there are higher chances that the borrower will fall behind on payments (for example, with debt from credit cards or payday loans).

Loan to value (LTV)

When people borrow money from the bank to buy a property, they need to borrow a certain percentage of the property asking price to fund the purchase. For example, if the asking price is £100,000 and you have £25,000 deposit to put towards the purchase, you will need to borrow £75,000 from the bank (or a kind friend) to be able to buy the property. In other words, you need a 75% loan to value mortgage.

LTV = amount borrowed/purchase price

To calculate the cost of your mortgage interest, you can use an assumed annual interest rate of 5% and assume that every £100,000 borrowed costs £5,000 per year (£416.66 per month).

Mortgage interest

There are lots of different mortgage products available and the best person to advise you on these is a mortgage broker. However, at the most basic level a mortgage payment will consist of the interest on the loan with or without a small capital repayment. For residential purchases, you almost always pay the interest plus a small repayment on the loan every month. For investment purchases, many people opt for interest-only mortgages to better leverage their funds elsewhere. This means they are not actively paying off the loan, just the interest which is calculated as follows:

Annual interest = amount borrowed x interest rate

For example, if my mortgage interest rate is 5% per annum and I need to borrow £100,000:

Annual interest = £100,000 x 5% = £5,000 per annum

Note that the interest may be calculated using the Bank of England (BOE) base rate plus an additional rate for the loan. Most mortgages will also have other fees at the start and end of the loan period which your broker will advise you of.

When choosing a mortgage there are some basic points to consider:

Early redemption/repayment charges (ERCs)

Mortgage product fee

Bank valuation fee

Admin fees

Exit fees (if you sell your house or want to repay the loan)

Whether there's a fixed term rate and, if so, the interest rate after the fixed term

Another important consideration is that in order for the bank to lend you the desired amount for an investment property, the market rental income of the property must be 25-50% higher than the estimated mortgage interest payment. You can calculate this as follows:

Target rent = mortgage interest x 1.25

Using the example above, if you need to borrow £100,000 at 5% per year which would result in a mortgage interest cost of £5,000 per year, you need the market rent to be at least £6,250.

For example, *target rent = £5,000 x 1.25 = £6,250*

TOP TIP

Aim for your rental income to be double the cost of your mortgage but use a spreadsheet to stress-test your project at different rates of interest so you can understand at which point the deal stops working.

Yield

The next concept to get your head around is yield, as it is widely used as a general indicator of the income (profit) generating performance of a property as an asset relative to its value. To calculate rental yield, you need to know the *annual rent* and the *value or purchase price of the property.*

Annual rent = weekly rent x 52

Yield is calculated by dividing the rental income generated by the value of the property to understand the profit generated as a percentage of the property's value.

$$\text{Yield} = \frac{\text{rental income}}{\text{property value}} \times 100$$

If a property worth £100,000 can be rented out for £10,000 per annum, the yield is 10%. Once you understand the concept of yield, you can use it to compare the yield of single lets versus multi-lets, or to compare yields of properties in different geographical locations across the UK.

However, you must bear in mind that many estate agents will be advertising the gross yields, calculated using gross rents—they will not have allowed for expenses such as mortgage payments, service charges, void periods (periods of time when a property might be empty and not generating rental income), or insurance. These will vary depending on the investor's circumstances (and also drive down the yield and make the property investment look less attractive!). In London, it's common to see single-let properties advertised as having a gross rental yield of 5-6%, while in reality (if using a mortgage and considering other expenses) the yield is far more likely to be around the 1-2% mark after rental expenses are accounted for. It is up to you to do the calculations based on your personal circumstances and decide what sort of a yield is attractive to you.

Return on investment (ROI), return on cash invested (ROCI) and return on capital employed (ROCE)

While yield can be a useful as a general guide of how well an asset is performing, unless you're buying in cash it doesn't give you a clear picture of how hard your personal cash or funds invested into the deal are working.

For this reason, many people like to use return on investment (ROI), return on cash invested (ROCI) or return on capital employed (ROCE) as these tell you the return or profit you get from the cash that you (or your investors) have invested in the project after costs. These terms are frequently used interchangeably, so check what someone means when they use the term and how they have calculated it. Generally, the concept is the same and throughout this book I'll stick to using ROI. The ROI is the pre-tax return or profit you get from the cash you have invested in the project after costs. The cash invested in the project will include the deposit, purchasing and any refurbishment expenses. As above, be aware of gross and net ROI. I always calculate pre-tax net ROI (as tax will vary depending on individual circumstances), so I'll do the same here.

The ROI is calculated as a percentage by dividing the pre-tax profits (income minus expenses) by the actual cash invested in the deal (deposit, refurb, legal costs etc.).

$$ROI = \frac{income - costs}{cash\ invested} \times 100$$

Using a simplified example of a property worth £100,000 which can be rented out for £10,000 a year, let's imagine we have a deposit of £25,000 and buy with a mortgage of £75,000 at an interest rate of 3% per year. The mortgage interest alone costs us £2250 per annum. Therefore, the ROI for the funds invested in this property is as follows:

$$ROI = \frac{£10{,}000 - £2{,}250}{£25{,}000} \times 100$$

ROI = 31%

Can you see how much of a difference it makes using the ROI to assess how hard your money is working for you? Take a moment to reflect on how well your hard-earned funds might be working for you *right now* whether that is your savings in the bank, your pension, an ISA, or any other investments. Is it working harder than the current rate of inflation? Do you think you might be able to make your money work way harder for you through investing in property? I am sure it can, and I hope by the end of this book you'll agree with me.

In reality there are many more expenses to consider when buying, developing, or renting out a property. You should always account for as many expenses as possible (expected and unexpected) to accurately assess a deal and prevent any unwelcome surprises after purchase. Unexpected costs can quickly eat away at your profits, and it is crucial to recognise them not only when you are searching for a good deal yourself, but also if you are presenting the deal to a joint venture partner.

Take a look at some of the most common expenses property investors consider when analysing a deal below:

Purchase expenses
Survey fees
Solicitor's conveyancing fees
Lease extension fees
Mortgage valuation fee
Mortgage product arrangement fee
Mortgage broker fee
Stamp duty
Refurbishment expenses
Cost of refurbishment (labour and materials)
15-20% contingency for unexpected costs
Mortgage interest payments
Utilities and service charges during rental voids
Project manager fees
Cleaners
Rental expenses
Lettings agency fees
Management fees
Mortgage interest fees
Content insurance
Buildings insurance
Landlord accreditation
Landlord insurance
Rental protection insurance
Service charges and ground rent
Rental voids
Maintenance

As you can see, there are many expenses to include in your assessment and I suggest you create a simple 'deal analyser' spreadsheet that will help you to assess every deal you come across. There is no right/wrong way to do this, as the criteria will vary depending on the type of property you want to invest in. Most likely you will end up with several different spreadsheets to use for different kinds of property projects. The most important thing is to be realistic and thorough in your appraisals.

TOP TIP

Always ensure you are in profit after all expenses are deducted and don't forget to account for income tax at your personal tax rate.

How to work out if a property is a good deal

Knowing whether the property you are looking at is a good deal or not is an issue that causes many people considerable anxiety and indecision, but it ultimately comes down to calculating your ROI or yield and ensuring the property is generating a good profit after costs. This means ensuring you account for all costs involved in your project whether it is a buy to let or you are buying, refurbishing and selling.

As mentioned earlier, an easy benchmark to use is how hard your cash is working right now. Aim for an investment that will make your cash work harder (taking into account what sort of risk is reasonable to you). The great thing about property is that you can be aware of and understand the risks prior to investing (as discussed in Chapter 3) and use different strategies to 'de-risk' your investment as far as possible.

If you have felt anxious about this, you will be glad to hear that strictly speaking there is no right or wrong answer as it is up to you to decide what sort of profits you want to make from property and set the investment criteria that seem suitable to you. Investors in London may be happy with yields of 3-5% whereas people investing in the north of England may only be satisfied with yields over 12%. Investors who use ROI to guide their decisions may look at anything from 7% to 25% or more, depending on their personal requirements, appetite for risk and duration of the project. Generally speaking, investments with higher returns are more likely to be higher risk or require higher maintenance to run and manage. If you are a beginner to property investment, you might find the below useful:

For each property investment or project you look at, consider:

1. Does it generate a profit? (Your investment should ALWAYS be profit generating after all costs. If it isn't, find a way to enable it to generate profits or move on.) If you buy using a mortgage the bank will usually require the rental income to be 25% higher than the cost of estimated mortgage interest.

2. What is the yield, ROI and cash flow after costs? (How hard your cash will work in this deal must be better than what you are getting in the bank, whether you are buying for the long term or selling in the short term).

3. Does it fit your strategy or goals? (Is it helping you get where you want to go? If not, why are you doing it?)

4. Is it worth your time? (make sure you get a good return on your time invested.)

5. Do you have good enough exit strategies? (What if you cannot achieve the desired outcome? Can you generate profit in a different way?)

6. Are you buying at the right price (ideally below market value)? You should always try to lock in profit from the start (we will discuss this in more detail in the next section).

In summary, when appraising a deal to see whether it makes sense you should ensure it is cash-flow positive, and it satisfies your ROI or rental yield criteria. Every investor will have different criteria in terms of what ROI or rental yield they want to achieve. Bear in mind that different strategies will give different returns. As a baseline, think about what your money could currently get by leaving it sitting in the bank and explore whether you can beat that by investing it yourself or by working with someone else. Choose your criteria and find a deal that suits your needs.

Market value

Market value is dictated by the price the target market is willing to pay to rent or buy a property, be it buyers or tenants! It is important to know what the market rental or sales value of a property is both when buying and selling a property to understand whether a property is priced below market value, or over market value. For every project you assess, you should have a list of comparables (properties that are similar in price, size and location to the property you are considering investing in). Record the size, price, condition, rental and sales value of these comparable properties. This will help you to quickly get a sense of the market value for properties in the area and value for money. You will also be able to compare and contrast unmodernised and refurbished properties, which is important if your project is a doer-upper that you will be selling on or refinancing as you will need certainty on profit margins.

You can easily research market values by doing a quick search on Rightmove.com, Zoopla.com or any other property portal. To be sure, call a few agents and ask them how much they let or sold their last few properties for (you may find the price agreed differs from the price advertised online and this will save you from making costly mistakes). Some agents are helpful and will send you a list of properties recently let or sold, including the dates and addresses.

This is the best proof or evidence that you can get of what a property is worth. For sales values, some online property platforms will show you the *sold* prices while others will give an estimated value—ignore estimates as these are rarely accurate and are often way out! If you want to take things a step further and *really* test the market, create a few dummy adverts (of your property for sale or rent) at different price points and measure responses to the adverts over a period of one or two weeks. You will soon get a feel for demand and market value whether it is for sales or rental properties.

Below market value (BMV) properties

What about below market value (BMV) properties? Once you determine what the market value is you will know whether a property is being sold below market value or not. But how much below market value is enough? Typically, you should aim for properties priced 20% BMV to get a good saving/locked in profit. Some people can negotiate more or source properties that are heavily discounted for a number of reasons (including death, divorce or damage) that would make someone want to sell fast or at a low price to get rid of it and move on. The recent Section 24 changes and Brexit woes have certainly contributed towards some landlords and property owners throwing in the towel.

Many BMV properties are sourced from motivated sellers, some of whom are desperate or vulnerable and get preyed on by unethical investors. While you should look after your business interests, you should always try to find an ethical solution that works for both parties. As doctors this may come more easily since we work with vulnerable people every day and, fortunately for NHS workers, our work decisions are based on clinical need and not on profits. If you do enter the world of property, make sure you apply the ethics and values learnt in healthcare to your property business as well.

Where to buy

People often ask me where they should buy their investment property, which areas are best to invest in and where the most in-demand locations are. This is a difficult question to answer unless you have good knowledge of a particular area or have done some decent research. The area you invest in will also depend on your particular strategy. For example, if you are interested in boutique holiday lets in the countryside, a rural area popular for country walks and outdoor activities may be perfect.

You can find some good reports and analyses of the UK property market available online or in property magazines. These reports often give up to date data on property prices and yields nationwide.

In large cities like London you can find reports of how boroughs throughout the city are performing (by rental yield or average sales price) and whether prices are going up or down, as well as information on key areas where values are expected to rise However, there is nothing like having (or getting access to) local knowledge about a particular property market as it will help you understand supply and demand and any current or future push and pull factors such as re-development (for example, shopping centres, new tube stations or parks).

Narrowing it down

To help narrow down your search, particularly when you are trying to compare two or more areas, you can use the data available on the property portals. Like when you are searching for a property, pre-select the type, price and area of the property you include in your search criteria and the radius within which you want to capture results. Then you need complete the following steps:

Using properties for sale as an example:

1. Take note of the number of properties for sale found using your chosen criteria.
2. Do the same search again, this time clicking the sold subject to contract (SSTC) option. Properties listed as SSTC have recently gone under offer but are not necessarily sold. Using these criteria means you now have the total number of properties available in an area, including those under offer.
3. Divide the number for sale by the total number available to get an idea of available stock relative to total number of properties on the market:

$$\%\ \textit{available properties} = \frac{\textit{properties for sale}}{\textit{properties for sale} + \textit{properties SSTC}}$$

Calculating this as a percentage allows you to compare areas you are thinking about investing in.

4. If Area 1 has 80% of available properties for sale and Area 2 has just 20% of available properties for sale, you can quickly understand that Area 2 is a more desirable place to live as reflected by a lack of available stock (people either don't sell very often, or when properties do come onto the market they sell fast).

The above method can also be used to assess supply and demand in the rental market. However, it is a rough way to assess demand in a given area and data available online may not be up to date. For example, some properties may be listed more than once if they are for sale with different agents, leading to inaccuracies.

Other ways to assess demand and supply are to ask estate agents and lettings agents for figures on number of properties listed versus number of applicants searching, or to place dummy adverts online of your own to assess demand.

Doctor's orders: General rules to keep you out of trouble

Use the acronym DOCTOR to remember some simple criteria to follow when investing in a BTL property (as well as a number of others). Some of these may already be obvious to you but will hopefully serve to reassure you that the so-called 'golden rules' of investing are based on common sense. The challenge for most people is when it comes to implementing these rules and being disciplined about what property deals you will accept or reject. Stick to the below criteria in addition to your **personal investment criteria such as ROI and yield** and you should minimise your risk and maximise your returns!

DOCTOR

D is for Development

Try to buy properties with development potential or the possibility to add value in some way. This could vary from a simple cosmetic refurbishment to carrying out a loft conversion or extension or dramatically altering the layout of the property. More experienced investors may consider adding value to existing buildings or land through conversions or building projects.

O is for Old

It is easier to assess the market value of older properties due to the fact there is more historical data available. Also, a lot of people LOVE a period property and the original features inside (in some cities period properties are significantly more expensive than comparable properties in mansion blocks or new developments due to their desirability). Bear in mind that this is not the case everywhere (for example many foreign buyers prefer new builds) and depending on your target outcome (rent or sell), this may or may not be an important factor.

C is for Cash flow and Cheap

Obvious again, right? Wrong. So many people don't do enough due diligence and buy properties that yield little or no cash flow or that over the years start to cash flow negatively. Always buy a property that will have *strong* cash flow. Ideally, your property should also be *below market value*, and there are many ways to find properties below market value. Aim for 15-20% BMV as it locks in a profit and safety net against a decrease in market value (for example, a market crash). If you are buying below market value, you are already making a profit at purchase and hence have some equity locked in and protection against a falling property market from the outset.

T is for Transport and amenities

Most people want to live in a place that is convenient for their work and lifestyle. Again, local knowledge is important. For example, in my area people generally do not want to have to walk more than ten to fifteen minutes to get to a tube station or supermarket and they hardly use cars. In rural places like Wales where I grew up, public transport is infrequent, so being close to a tube or bus stop is much less of an issue as most people drive.

O is for Options

It's good to have options, and what I'm referring to here is having as many ways as possible to create a profitable investment whether through single let, multi-let, refurbishing and selling the property or adding value then releasing equity. You cannot control market conditions, but you can predict and plan for the worst. Every time you look at property that suits your strategy try to come up with a plan for what you might do if you are unable to implement your strategy and whether this would be a complete disaster or not. For example, if you buy an HMO think about what you might do if you later find you are unable to use it as an HMO. Would letting it as a single-let cover the mortgage? Could you sell for a profit? It is good practice to think through these scenarios and better still to formally appraise the different options.

R is for Rental Demand

Always buy in an area with strong rental demand. This is most important if you are letting the property and need tenants to pay you the rent that will cover the mortgage! It's also important if you are developing a property to sell to a BTL investor. You can assess the rental demand in an area as mentioned previously, but you can also use some fool-proof techniques I learned as a landlord and which we will cover in Chapter 9.

You can also use the acronym ADOPE as a reminder of properties you should approach with caution unless you are very experienced, understand the local market and have the skills, resources and network to deal with them.

ADOPE

A is for buying Abroad

Buying abroad can be as profitable as buying in the UK but there are factors to consider such as local currency and exchange rates, whether you have adequate knowledge of the local market, whether you have a team to call on if there are tenant or maintenance issues and whether there are there mortgage or tax hurdles to overcome. The last thing you want to do when starting out is to create extra stress or problems for yourself, so make sure you consider investments abroad carefully and seek the support of an expert where appropriate.

D is for Dilapidated properties

By dilapidated I don't mean properties that need a complete refurb, I mean properties with serious structural problems that may be above and beyond the scope of your time, budget or experience level. Such properties may even need to be knocked down! A bargain property can quickly turn into a nightmare project if you buy such a property on a whim without properly assessing it. To avoid this, always ensure you conduct a building survey and get appropriate building and construction professionals to quote for works prior to purchase.

O is for off-plan or new build

I won't go into this in too much detail here as it is covered in Chapter 10 (including a case study on how you can successfully invest in new builds and off plan projects). However, the main reasons to be cautious are that it is often difficult to assess the market value of a brand-new property due to the fact that there may be no like-for-like comparables. If a property has not been built yet, you will need intricate knowledge of the local property market to understand what the value will be by the time it is built. You will also need to consider the strength of the local market and the track record of the developer to ensure they do not go bust in the process.

P is for Poor location

Finding the right property in the right location for your strategy is of the utmost importance. For example, don't set up an HMO in the middle of nowhere as young professionals usually want to live close to where they work and within walking distance of amenities such as public transport and supermarkets. Likewise, an eco-tourism holiday home would likely work best in an areas of outstanding natural beauty. Make sure your property will be appealing to the market you are targeting. This is common sense.

E is for Expensive

For the reasons discussed in this chapter previously, expensive properties are usually not worth buying unless you have big plans to maximise the cash flow or add value in some way which boosts the market value of the property. Buying a property over-market value can often mean driving down your rental yield or your ROI so take care to calculate the maximum price at which your project works and do not go over this.

TOP TIPS

Gain a clear understanding of different investment terms and never be afraid to ask for clarification when unsure.

Decide on investment criteria that suit your needs using yield, ROI, cash flow or equity gain.

Use DOCTOR and ADOPE in addition to your investment criteria, to assess potential investments.

Create a deal analyser with income and expenses to evaluate potential investments.

CHAPTER 5

THE BIG 5 INVESTMENT STRATEGIES AND HOW TO DEVELOP YOURS

Having a plan when it comes to property investment is vital. It's similar to setting up a business or even becoming a doctor—you're unlikely to succeed if you set out without a plan or identifying the steps you need to take to achieve your goals. Having a clear plan will help you clarify your goals and identify the kinds of investments or property strategies that will help you achieve them. To do this, you need to know as much as possible about the different ways in which you can invest in property, choose a strategy and focus on it. If you don't want to do that, you can try the 70:20:10 rule where you choose three strategies that fit with your needs, but spend the majority of your time focusing on the most important ones that will help you reach your goals.

This chapter outlines the most common and popular strategies currently used by property investors and will give you a good flavour of the creative and exciting strategies available for you to use to help you to reach your goals.

Buy to let

Buy to let is easily the most common property strategy known and the basic model implies buying a property to let it out, usually to a single tenant, long-term (for example, six to twelve months). Technically speaking, any property purchased to let out is a buy-to-let, but depending on the type and number of tenants and the duration of the tenancy, the name given to the type of letting differs. For example, when you let a property, you can choose to let it in one of the following ways (subject to local rules and regulations as well as your mortgage terms and conditions): single let; serviced accommodation; holiday let; multi-let (for example, HMOs); and commercial let (to shops or companies). These may be long lets (over three months) or short lets (anything up to ninety days). Different types of letting require different types of rental agreements, so make sure you check with a solicitor or relevant authority before going ahead.

You might want to consider investing in a BTL if life is too unstable for you to settle on investing in a property where you will live long term. You might also consider BTL if you can't afford to buy in the area you want to live yet. The income from a BTL might offset the cost of renting in your desired area, anyway. The affordability of a BTL mortgage is calculated based on the rental income the property can generate in addition to your salary while residential mortgage affordability is exclusively based on your salary and spending habits. These days, it's sometimes easier to get a BTL mortgage than a residential mortgage, while traditionally it was thought you could not get a BTL mortgage as a FTB. Times have definitely changed and there has been a significant increase in appetite from the banks for lending to FTB on a BTL basis.

So back to the basic BTL model: you buy a property and rent it out to make a profit—simple, right? Wrong. Having taught and spoken to hundreds of doctors about property, I'm shocked by how many doctors have bought a buy to let property using few or zero criteria, and without knowing how to calculate whether a deal makes sense or not. The result is that many more people than you might imagine own buy to let properties which either yield little profit, or worse still, they make a loss every month (this happens when expenses are higher than rental income). This can happen for a number of reasons including being on a suboptimal mortgage product; making loan repayments as well as mortgage interest payments; void periods; drop in market rent; rise in interest rates and (more recently) Section 24.

You may be thinking *What about capital growth? People don't just buy for cash flow.* Of course, this should be considered and balanced with any profits or losses from rental income, but capital growth is a long term game and shouldn't be relied on. More to the point, there are far too many profitable investments out there which can provide a strong rental income as well as capital appreciation in the long term (or the short term if you're adding value to the property). There's no reason for you to invest in a troublesome asset if you follow some simple rules and get your numbers right.

If you're in this situation, immediately re-evaluate the property and assess whether there is a way for you to maximise the cash flow or increase its value. If you can't make the property profitable, you may want to consider cutting your losses by selling up and ensuring you make a much better investment next time. If you're in the position of selling at a small loss, weigh this up against holding the property (potentially at a loss for another few years). If either way you're making a loss, it may be time to face reality, accept you made some mistakes and make sure you do better next time.

If you can work out whether a deal stacks up or not, and understand the principles of cash flow, return on investment and rental yield, this will stand you in good stead for picking a strategy that works for you and taking decisive action whether it's BTL or other strategies. This is exactly what Dr Cat Davison did when she decided to invest in BTLs. Within a year she had built a portfolio of high yield properties despite not living in the UK at that time!

CASE STUDY

Dr Cat Davison, military GP who since working in South Sudan with the United Nations has managed to buy five houses in the last year

My mother had been trying to push me to try a property course for some time, and I'd resisted as I thought it would be a con and a sales pitch. Before going on the course, I had a coaching session with Lafina at Eurekadoc who helped me clarify my goals and work out which strategies to use. Shortly afterwards I signed up for a starter course and learnt so much about different strategies that I signed up for another course straight away.

That was a year ago and since then I've met many like-minded people through my property network and hit it off with Emerald, my now business partner. We joined forces and set up a business with the aim of investing in high yield single lets. It really was jump right in and go for it. We started looking for property in the Cotswolds, close to both our homes, but quickly realised if we wanted to be successful at single buy to lets, the bread and butter of many an investor, we would have to move north of Coventry or west, past Bristol. Therefore, Emerald moved to Liverpool to start sourcing the properties while I continued in full-time military service.

It's not been easy; everything happens more slowly than you want, and you do make mistakes. Ours have ranged from not sticking to one strategy, thus wasting time, to moving areas too frequently resulting in missing opportunities when they come up—it takes time to build contacts and a pipeline and it's worth waiting for the fruits of your labour. We wish we'd become good at one thing, which would have allowed us to have grown quicker rather than trying to chase the shiny pennies. However, through working with our joint venture partner Nigel we bought single buy to lets in Liverpool and St Helens in cash for £40-£50K.

They are houses we purchased pre-auction or through direct to vendor marketing and are to be refurbished, tenanted with a family and re-mortgaged to pull money out.

I'm currently away on a nine-month tour in South Sudan, which we knew I would be doing when we formed the company. As I'm writing this case study for you, Emerald has moved to Liverpool and is living and estate agents, nurturing relationships and sourcing deals while I'm sitting on the internet training Erin, our virtual assistant, to write our operational manuals and do the tasks we don't have time for to try to get us organised and efficient.

We have a potential development site in the pipeline and that is what we really want to do, apart from being more philanthropic and giving back to support the homeless. I would love to leave the military and make property my job; we've given ourselves five years to replace my income.

We have one life, we must live it.

TOP TIPS

Define your investment criteria

Select the type of BTL, number of tenants and duration of letting

Consult a broker to find the most appropriate mortgage

Take action and cut your teeth on a small project. Some like to start big but making mistakes on small projects is less costly than on big ones!

Save 20% of your net pre-tax profits every month towards your tax bill.

Invest for cash flow, not just capital appreciation!

In addition to their own cash deposit, many people will use a mortgage to invest in buy to let properties but there are always people who can or prefer to buy without using bank loans using completely their own (or someone else's) cash. If you are using a mortgage, it's critical that you work out whether the rental income from the property will cover the mortgage payments. We will use an easy example assuming we are purchasing with a 75% loan to value (LTV) mortgage.

Purchase price £100,000

25% deposit £25,000

75% loan £75,000

At present, BTL mortgage interest rates are around 3% per annum, so for every £100,000 you borrow it will cost you £3,000 per year (£250 per month). In the example above, we borrow £75,000 from the bank at a cost of £2,250 per year (£187.50 per month).

For the bank to lend to you, they will require a market rent of 1.25 times the quoted mortgage interest as a minimum. In some cases, it will need to be 1.5 times greater and they also take your salary into account. So if your mortgage interest is £187.50, you'll need to ensure you can prove a market rent for this type of property of at least £234.38, leaving you with £46.88 profit. If the current market rents are above this, the lender is likely to agree the mortgage. If the current market rents are below it, they will probably not approve your application. Personally, I would always ensure that your expected rental income is 1.5 to two times greater than the mortgage interest to cover your expenses and leave you with a cash buffer for emergencies as well as rental profits.

The above example is grossly simplified as there are many other expenses you must account for when calculating whether a deal stacks up or not. These may include refurbishment costs; maintenance costs; landlord insurance; lettings agent fees; service charges and even void periods where you may have an empty property with no rent coming in. If you want to make a conservative estimate for voids, calculate eleven months of rent as a worst-case scenario (if you're organised and price your property correctly, you should hardly ever have voids).

Here's an example of how one of my single let properties in London performs on a monthly basis rented out to a single tenant on a long-term contract, luckily this one is let on a long contract, so I haven't had any voids for several years:

Single let example, London

Rental income: £2,120

Mortgage £700

Service charges £340

Agent fees £200

Landlord insurance £10

Pre-tax profits £880

The rental income in this example is three times the mortgage interest which more than satisfies the bank's criteria for lending. Once you understand how to quickly analyse whether a deal works or not, you can apply it to lots of different strategies as the concept is always the same in understanding whether a deal is profitable or not: income – expenses = profit.

Buy, refurbish, refinance (BRR)

This, as the name indicates, involves buying a property, refurbishing it to add value (therefore increasing the market value of the property) and refinancing it (ideally, to extract all or most of the original funds invested and use them to invest again). Investors like BRR as it means they can keep recycling their funds from one project to another which allows them to build up a portfolio of investment properties quite quickly. This method is also called *momentum investing* and works best with properties priced under £100,000 due to low stamp duty costs, although you can use this strategy on any project if the numbers work. While you can use mortgages to purchase properties under £100,000 bear in mind that you will have limited options in getting a mortgage for properties under £40,000, and you may have to wait a minimum of six to twelve months before your lender will release further funds to you. Below is an example of how BRR can work for a cash purchase.

Imagine you find a cheap property for £60,000 that needs refurbishment. The refurbishment work, and legal fees will cost you approximately £30,000 but you know that similar refurbished properties have been selling for £130,000. You buy the property in cash and refurbish it, spending £90,000 in total.

After the work is done you have it valued at £130,000. You could either sell the property and pay tax on the £40,000 profit or you could refinance it. If you're granted a 75% LTV mortgage on the property based on its current value of £130,000, you'll receive £97,500 as a loan upon equity release (this would cover your initial capital invested of £90,000 AND give you £7,500 extra funds to invest in your next property). Better still, you would still have £32,500 equity left in the property. You then rent the property out to tenants; the rental income covers your mortgage and hey presto, you've got yourself a great investment! In theory (and assuming a major economic crisis doesn't occur), if you hold onto that property for long enough, it will increase in value. During this time, you could re-finance more equity out to invest in more properties, or you could pay down the mortgage and enjoy an asset that will produce a good income.

You can use the BRR strategy on practically any property type ranging from any type of residential to commercial properties. What is key to being successful is buying at the right price, or increasing the value of the property through refurbishment enough to boost its value and allow you to refinance out your original funds. For some deals this could range from carrying out a light cosmetic improvement to doing a loft conversion, to developing an office building into flats and refinancing the new product. But how do you know what the right price to buy at is? Well, you apply the simple calculation below which assumes you will refinance using a 75% loan to value mortgage (but you can modify the calculation to account for different LTVs).

$$\text{Maximum purchase price} = \frac{(\text{target end value x } 75\%) - (\text{refurb and legal fees})}{1.03^{*}}$$

*1.03 is used to factor in the SDLT payable at 3%. However, feel free to alter this to reflect the level of SDLT you would pay on more expensive properties.

Using the above example, the maximum price we should pay for the property would be calculated as follows:

$$\text{Maximum purchase price} = \frac{(\pounds 130{,}000 \text{ x } 75\%) - (\pounds 30{,}000)}{1.03^{*}} = \pounds 65{,}533$$

TOP TIPS

Ensure your project fits the above formula unless you are willing to leave some cash in the deal.

To get a great post-works valuation, prepare a report for the valuer including purchase price, cost of refurbishment, floorplans and lists of comparable properties in poor and good condition.

Have a contingency plan in case you do not get your desired valuation or cannot refinance out the desired amount of cash.

Rent to rent (R2R)

Rent to rent is a favourite strategy among many investors who don't have any cash to invest as it allows you to use leverage to make massive cash flow from a property without buying it. (It's also known as let-to-let, let to multi-let, corporate letting, leasing and many other variations.) This strategy works by renting out a property for a period of three to five years or more and legally subletting it to a tenant(s) to generate a positive cash flow (after expenses). Naturally, the rent you receive from your tenant must be greater than the rent you pay to the owner of the property (just like when you have a mortgage) and any expenses you will be covering.

Why would a property owner consider allowing you to do this when they could do it themselves and keep the profits? Well, there are many landlords out there (both amateur and professional) who are tired of dealing with tenants and maintenance issues and would love someone to look after things while still paying them a good rent. There are a number of ways to negotiate a rent to rent deal, and they will vary depending on what's agreed between the landlord and yourself. The main elements to consider in your negotiations are:

Guaranteed rent to the landlord

No voids for the landlord as you're responsible for paying the rent

You may sublet the property to tenants (using an appropriate rental agreement called a management agreement or a lease agreement—do not use an assured shorthold tenancy [AST] for R2R—that's illegal)

You fully manage the property and cover maintenance costs, utilities, cleaning etc. up to an agreed monthly limit

You can make cosmetic improvements to the property (with the owner's consent)

The terms and conditions of the landlord's mortgage

- Appropriate home insurance covering plumbing, electrical and heating issues
- Taking out your own business insurance

Think about how you can best help the owner while creating a viable business for yourself. You may be wondering how you can make a profit if you are offering to pay the market rent. This is where the skills you'll develop in assessing how to maximise the potential of a property come in. You might find that the landlord will be willing to rent it to you for a little below the market rent given that the luxury of having a fully managed property with no voids is far more valuable. The property can be used for long or short lets, depending on the type of property (commercial versus residential), the rules and regulations of the local council, the landlord's mortgage terms and conditions, health and safety factors and whether the landlord agrees in the first place. For example, you could use R2R to create cash flow from:

- A HMO property
- A serviced accommodation property
- Holiday letting
- Storage units
- Co-working spaces
- Alternative therapy centre
- Events spaces
- Car parks

If you're a creative problem-solver, you'll be able to think of far more situations in which you can rent a property and create an income from it. Be aware that if you are changing the use of the property you may need to apply for change of use with the council. If in doubt, always check with the council as you could run into trouble if the use of the property breaches planning laws. You should also be aware that business rates may be payable depending on the use and planning category the property falls into.

Dr Rachael Coates implemented the rent to rent strategy impressively, using it to scale a serviced accommodation business generating over £9,000 in revenue per month in north Yorkshire! Serviced accommodation refers to fully-furnished accommodation available for both short-term or long-term stays but with services included such as utilities, regular cleaning, bed linen and other hotel-like amenities. Rachael started with little prior experience and is a great example of how this strategy can work anywhere in the UK, provided that you know your market and get your numbers right.

CASE STUDY

Dr Rachael Coates: ST5 in general surgery with a transplant interest from Middlesbrough

Rachael had owned and refurbished a couple of properties and had always been interested in property investment and development, so while on maternity leave she set out to learn more. She read books, attended property events, and also joined a property sourcing mentoring programme designed to help her to set up her own property sourcing business. It was a low-risk and low outlay strategy that focused on sourcing properties direct to vendor. Her first couple of deals were ideal for rent to rent but at that stage she didn't have the network to sell them on so decided to do them herself! Having discovered the serviced accommodation (SA) strategy she realised that the deals she was sourcing in Middlesbrough would work perfectly!

Her first deals were classic two up, two downs (two-bed terraced houses with two reception rooms), approximately 57-65 m2 that would sleep up to six people (using sofa beds and single beds in some of the rooms). Both properties were unencumbered (mortgage-free). The rent she paid to the landlord was £375 per month agreed for a five-year period (the market rent was £450/month) and she did this using a management agreement that allowed her to sublet the rooms through the serviced accommodation model.

With serviced accommodation you have to be aware of local laws and regulations around short term lets. One of the requirements in Rachael's area is for her to pay business rates to the council (calculated by the number of beds in the property) which costs around £1,400 per year. Approximate monthly utilities cost as follows: water £40, gas and electricity £100-150, broadband £30.

Rachael rents these properties out for £69 per night plus £25 cleaning fee, resulting in a rental income of £1,500-1,800 gross and £400-700 net per month depending on the number of longer stays versus single night stays (which are more costly due to higher turnover on bed linen, cleaning etc.). Using this strategy, Rachael went from zero to turning over £8,000–9,000 gross per month in just seven months.

Rachael says that her experience in property has led to her becoming much more engaged with tech, both in property and medicine. She now sees ways of transferring the skills she has developed in business to medicine, and even though she is busier than ever before she uses her time more effectively and gets more done! Having a virtual assistant (VA) has helped, and doing the systems and outsourcing course of fellow investor-doctor Steve Day enabled Rachael to communicate and delegate effectively.

However, the real game changer has been the impact that entering the property investment world has had on her mindset. She told us, 'I'm not interested in private work. My income isn't limited by how many hours I work, anymore. I work as a doctor because it's something I love and I don't have to get involved in politics at work. At the end of the day,

R2R is sometimes perceived negatively due to the subletting aspect and the fact that unprofessional people have done and probably still do this illegally, either by using the wrong type of contract or without having the landlord's consent to sublet. However, if you do it legally and professionally, and always try to have the best interests of your landlord in mind as well as your own, not only is it a viable and profitable business but many interesting opportunities start to come your way. For example, I used this strategy in West London to rent a terraced house that I converted into a small multi-let property.

Over the years I developed a good relationship with the owners who appreciated the good care I took of their property and professionalism with which I dealt with any issues. Because of this, the owners ended up offering me more properties to take on and we even ended up investing in a development project together.

Overall, R2R is a great way to quickly invest in property if you don't have deposit funds available to you or if you want to create strong cash flow to supplement or replace your income. Like any strategy, it's not without risk. For example, some areas can become over-saturated and this will drive prices down and competition up. If your profit margins are tight and you need to lower your rent, this can be damaging, particularly if you're tied into a rental contract for a long period. Having a good relationship with the property owner is imperative as the value of good communication and business relationships can't be overestimated. As a back-up you can work clauses into your contractual agreement to mitigate against this sort of risk, for example, having a break clause after a certain period of time which would allow you to end the contract.

Other benefits of using R2R are that you don't have to pay expensive stamp duty or legal fees, take out a mortgage, or worry about exposure to variable property prices (though you're clearly exposed to the lettings market, whichever market that is, so make sure you do your homework and brainstorm how to minimise risk, since you'll be committed to paying rent for quite some time).

TOP TIPS

Set your business up appropriately before trying to negotiate a R2R deal, for example, website, professional registrations, business cards, references etc.

Always make sure you use the correct contract and build in a break clause in the event you need to terminate sooner than expected.

Check the local rules and regulations related to the proposed use of the property.

Ensure you are not in breach of the vendor's mortgage terms and conditions.

Always have business insurance—you can use simplybusiness.com for a quote.

Houses of multiple occupation

HMOs (or *multi-lets)* have been around for a long time. At one point or another you may have lived in a HMO yourself as a student or young doctor; the official definition of a HMO for licensing purposes under the Housing Act 2004 is a property occupied by five or more people, forming two or more separate households.[13] To maximise the potential of the HMO (and create higher cash flow) an investor may let the property on a room-by-room basis with bills included, rather than having all tenants on the same contract splitting a single-let rent between them. This works well for people who don't know each other as it allows greater independence and flexibility than being tied into a contract with others.

13 You can read more about the HMO licensing rules which were updated in October 2018, here: 'House in multiple occupation licence,' HM Revenue and Customs https://www.gov.uk/house-in-multiple-occupation-licence (13 November 2018) [accessed 13 November 2018]

In some HMOs there are shared kitchen and bathroom facilities while in others the rooms are more like bedsits with a kitchenette and even ensuite bathroom. Usually, these sorts of rooms are priced at a premium as most people will pay extra for the luxury of having their own bathroom. The rental income generated from HMOs is much higher than you could achieve through letting the property out to a single tenant or family, but the amount you can charge per room or unit is very much driven by demand in your area (you can check demand and market room rents on websites such as spareroom.com). The total rental income for the number of rooms let should be significantly higher than the market rent for letting the entire property on a single-let basis to make it worth running.

When comparing the profits on a single versus multi-let, don't forget to include the expenses associated with running a HMO (for example, utility bills; mortgage; cleaner; insurance). While HMOs generate a higher cash flow, they also generate higher tenant turnover and maintenance issues, so you need to make sure you set up a team to deal with this.

FTB HMO strategy

You may know someone whose parents bought them a property while at medical school and rented out the rooms to their friends. The rental income (even at mates' rates) can often far surpass the cost of the mortgage, resulting not only in the lucky student living for free but also generating an income. Parents are happy as their child has a place to live with their friends with all costs covered. The property will increase in value over the years and can be sold or continue to be let to future generations of students.

Most parents will buy the property in their own names and transfer it to their children once they have started work. This is not tax efficient for a couple of reasons. Firstly, there may be inheritance tax to pay on the property and secondly there will be capital gains tax to pay if the property has increased in value and is later sold. It's far better (if possible) to buy the property in the name of the student with parents acting as guarantors. This way, if the property is ever sold, there will be no capital gains tax due as the property will have been the student's primary residence for a number of years and they can enjoy a tax-free windfall as capital gains tax is currently not applicable to their primary residence! Always consult an accountant and mortgage broker if your parents are thinking of buying a property for this purpose or if you're thinking of buying a property for your children.

HMO safety regulations

A higher number of tenants means higher wear and tear costs, maintenance issues and a higher risk of accidents. You'll need to make sure that your HMO is fit for purpose and fulfils health and safety criteria such as providing emergency lighting, smoke alarms, fire doors and more. Requirements vary from one council to another (or indeed the type of HMO you are creating), so it's best to check your local council's website or give them a call to ask about the required safety standards. This will not only ensure the highest level of safety for your tenants but will also allow you to plan any refurbishment projects.

Article 4

In April 2010 the government introduced legislation that meant in some areas a small family house occupied by between three and six unrelated sharers requires a landlord to gain planning permission from the council before they could let it as a small HMO (C4 class) having changed it from a family home (C3 class). In October 2010 they amended the legislation allowing landlords to make the change from C3 to C4 under a general permitted development order (GPDO)—i.e. without planning permission.

Great news, but they also gave local authorities the right to remove permission for a C3–C4 change in use by means of an Article 4 Direction which councils have used to limit the number of HMOs created across geographical areas. The bottom line is you always need to check your local council and area rules and regulations around HMOs before you set one up. If the address of the property you want to let as a small HMO is in an Article 4 area then you will not be permitted to change the use of the property from C3 to C4.

TOP TIPS

Check the HMO rules and regulations in your area before setting up an HMO

Ensure you comply with minimum health and safety standards; ideally go over and above these

Design the property and services with the target tenant market in mind

Work out how many rooms you need occupied to cover costs and at what occupancy your profit starts

Remember that HMOs are higher maintenance than single lets but offer much higher rewards

You can set up systems and team members to run your HMO so you don't have to manage it.

You can create different types of HMO based on the type of tenant you are want to rent to. The market rent will therefore vary, depending on the area, condition of the property and the price your target market is willing to pay.

HMO tenant types

Students

Council tenants

Blue collar workers

White collar workers

Young professionals

CASE STUDY

Dr Louise Hancock, trainee in occupational medicine working in industry

Louise's first property purchase was her home in 2013; a flat near Holloway Road in London. She later moved in with her partner and rented out her flat, becoming an 'accidental landlord'. By 2015, the flat had significantly risen in value and she was able to refinance it, releasing equity to invest in another property. Her family had a few investment properties and she had always been interested in investing to create an additional source of income.

Louise learnt about different property investment strategies through magazines and social media groups and a HMO conference in 2016 that kick-started her appetite to gain further knowledge and be held accountable for her goals. She joined a twelve-month mentoring programme run by a well-respected property investor and developed a network of trusted property investors who meet regularly to discuss their goals and progress.

After researching various areas across London, she viewed over 40 properties in East Croydon, where she decided to invest in her first HMO. Croydon seemed particularly attractive compared to London due to the higher yields, plans for significant redevelopment, and strong capital growth for the long-term. Upon viewing one property in East Croydon, her partner noticed another property on the same street with a for sale sign in the garden, that had not been marketed effectively online. It turned out to be a probate property in need of significant refurbishment and had been on the market for many months. This house was a two-up, two-down mid-terrace within walking distance of the main train station and amenities, giving it strong potential.

After analysing the deal, Louise and her partner made an offer, with a view to carrying out an extensive refurbishment to create a six-bed professional HMO and gaining solid development experience in the process. The property was purchased with a combination of their own capital and privately borrowed funds at a fixed interest rate.

The deal

Purchase price: £323k, negotiated down from £350k

Fees: £18k for stamp duty, survey and legal work

Refurb and borrowing costs: £180-190k for a double dormer loft conversion, single story extension, back-to-brick strip out, new bathrooms, kitchen, fully furnished house, fire alarm systems, all professional fees and mandatory licensing. Interest on borrowed capital.

Refurb timescales: 6-7 months, following 2 months for architectural work and change of use consents from the council

Revaluation: £545k re-valuation, which was refinanced on a limited company HMO mortgage, leaving in £100k of equity

Passive income: £20k annually (after mortgage interest payments, bills and letting fees). Equates to 20% ROI

Although the end result was a huge success with the rooms all achieving optimal rents due to their high spec, the project was not without its challenges. Despite all preparation, the importance of thorough due-diligence on contractors was brought home when the builders went out of business during the job, adding to the overall complexity and delivery timescales. Louise and her partner were seeking a challenge and certainly managed to overcome quite a significant one, whilst amassing a huge amount of technical refurbishment and HMO expertise. They are actively seeking new HMO opportunities, whilst working with partners to help them achieve great returns.

Purchase lease options (PLO)

Has anyone ever told you that you can invest in a property for £1? If so, it was probably in reference to purchase lease options or purchase options. This is a complicated topic and the aim here is to introduce you to the subject as opposed to teach you everything there is to know about purchase lease options. A commercial solicitor who is experienced in lease options is the best person to advise you.

In simple terms, a *purchase option* is a type of legal agreement that gives you the right to purchase a property at a pre-agreed price within an agreed time period but without the *obligation* to do so. The fee for the privilege of doing this is usually £1, but depending on the type of property deal it could be in the thousands. In other words, you can control a property without owning it, like in the R2R strategy. If we go a step further and you want to use the property to generate profit (as you do in R2R) you need a *purchase lease option* contract which will allow you to use the property as you wish in return for a monthly payment (*lease fee*). Like in R2R you can even refurbish the property if you have the owner's consent to do so. This strategy suits people who either don't have funds to invest or don't want to invest large amounts of funds into property, or those who for some reason can't get a mortgage to buy at that time.

The PLO strategy is relatively unknown to the general public but it is widely used by property developers and commercial investors. Typically, they use a purchase option to control a piece of land or building while applying for planning permission. A purchase option buys them time, minimises the risk of buying an asset where planning applications (which cost thousands) are rejected, and also temporarily eliminates competition as the vendor isn't permitted to sell to anyone else while under a LO contract.

CASE STUDY

Steeve Lamontagne, property investor and entrepreneur

My friend Steeve Lamontagne was looking for a house to rent that was closer to his son's school in the south-east. One day he came across a beautiful looking house with a for sale sign in the garden that advertised a mobile number to contact for more info. Steeve got lucky here as he ended up speaking to the owner directly, which is always far easier as you can sit down, have an honest conversation and see if you can make a deal work for both parties. It turned out the house had been empty for years and the owner (who owned several properties, had a busy life and was going through a divorce) had been paying out £2,000 a month on a mortgage. He was so busy that he didn't have the time or inclination to let the house and was now getting desperate. He wanted a price of £575,000 to sell the house but after some research Steeve discovered this was overpriced in the current market. Rather than buy an overpriced property, he decided to try and create a win-win situation by making the vendor a different offer. Steeve offered to rent the property for a couple of years, make some critical improvements using his own cash, and if he liked the property, he would buy it for £575,000 at the end of the term agreed. The owner was delighted and agreed. He even threw in the Land Rover that had been sitting unused on the drive for a few years!

Why would any property owner agree to do this?

It may be hard to believe, but there are lots of property owners who would consider a lease option, particularly in the current market. For example, a few years ago the property market was enjoying a boom period with high prices, lots of buyers and relatively little stock. At the time of writing this book, property prices have dropped and buyers have lost confidence in the market. Many buyers still want to sell but are unable to sell at the price they want or need. For example, selling at a lower value than when they purchased the property may mean losing money or not being able to pay off the mortgage. If the seller isn't desperate to sell, and price is more important to them than a quick sale, they may agree to a lease option as illustrated in Steeve's case study below.

You can control a property using a purchase lease option and use it in a number of ways to:

Buy a property BMV at some point in the future

Create massive cash flow using a multi-let strategy

De-risk your property development deals

Flip a property

Upgrade your current home

Although Steeve originally used the property to meet his accommodation needs, having his investment hat on he wanted to keep his options open. After the two-year option period he decided he wanted to move again, so instead of buying the property he decided to flip it. To his great surprise he had the property re-valued and thanks to the improvement works he had done it was valued at £795,000. One of the other benefits of using a lease option is that it can allow you to flip a property on for a higher price without the hassle of buying with a mortgage and wasting money on SDLT. This is done using an assignable contract where you, the buyer, have the right to assign the sale to a third party. In this way you can sell the property at a profit while satisfying your obligations to the seller without ever having purchased the property.

Here's the breakdown on Steeve's deal:

Purchase price £570,000

Refurbishment £70,000

Legal fees £1,000

Option fee £1

Lease fee £2,000 pcm approximately (Steeve considered it rent)

Option period 3 years

End valuation £795,000

Profit £153,999

How do you find a LO?

You may be wondering how you can find a lease option for yourself. There are a few ways that you can source LOs. Commonly, properties that are on both the sales and lettings market may be potential lease option deals but a LO deal may evolve in a natural manner throughout the negotiation problem solving process.

Negotiating with the owner or the agents

Negotiating a lease option deal can get tricky because a) most agents and vendors will never had heard of one and b) because if you don't know how to explain it in simple terms they will lose trust or feel it's too complicated! It's a good idea to get some negotiating tips from a fellow property investor or mentor who has experience with lease options.

1. Don't use the words 'lease option' with estate agents or vendors (unless, of course, they suggest this first). If they don't know what you're talking about, it may lead to a breakdown in communication.

2. Always try to meet the vendor in person, have a conversation with them about what is important to them, then try to create a solution that works for both parties.

3. Use simple language, for example, *Are you in a hurry to sell? Is the sale price more important to you than selling it fast? Can you be flexible about when you sell the property if you sell at your ideal price? Would you be interested in renting your property to me for a couple of years before I buy it?*

4. If you're communicating with a vendor through an agent or any third party, you should ideally use an agent you know and trust. Keep the message simple to avoid it becoming diluted or confused, and ideally give the agent a written offer to forward to the vendor.

5. Never ever cut an agent out of a deal. If you successfully negotiate a lease option, always pay the agent a sales commission fee. Business is about building relationships and you should always maintain an ethical approach, treating others in the way you would want to be treated.

What do you put in the contract?

If you're speaking directly with the vendor, you can create your own document with the terms you have agreed and send it to your solicitors to do the hard work! This is the *heads of terms* document, and sets out all of the key terms that yourself and the vendor have agreed upon such as:

Names and addresses of the parties involved (yourself and the vendor)

Address of the property

Agreed purchase price

Terms of the agreement

Monthly lease fee

Option fee (usually £1 but may be more)

Details of any works to be carried out with the owner's consent

A PLO agreement should be drawn up by a solicitor (ideally, a commercial solicitor, or one experienced in doing these kinds of agreements). You should always have two or three different solicitors you can call on to act for yourself and the vendor as it is likely that if the vendor uses a solicitor who has never heard of a lease option, it will either cause huge delays or the solicitor, having never heard of it, may err on the side of caution and advise against it.

TOP TIPS

PLOs are high leverage investments as you're able to maximise your gain for far less than you could by purchasing outright.

If you've never negotiated a PLO before, consider asking someone more experienced to help you.

Ensure you have a solicitor who understands PLOs and who can draw up suitable contracts.

Never take advantage of vulnerable people and always try to create a win-win solution for all.

There have been some concerns about using lease options on residential properties due to the fact that if the property suddenly rises steeply in value, despite having agreed a fixed price at the start of the contract, the vendor may feel hard done by or taken advantage of (even if at the time they had got the price they wanted and some great rental income in the meantime). However, LOs are legal and the most important thing is to ensure you and the vendor are given independent legal advice by qualified professionals at the time of agreeing the contract so you're aware of the implications of the contract. Furthermore, there's nothing stopping you from adapting the contract to include any terms agreed between yourself and the vendor until both parties are satisfied. Due to current Brexit uncertainty and tax changes, now is an ideal time to be negotiating lease options. What are you waiting for?

Freehold to leasehold and title splitting and building conversions

This is just a short note on a great way to create value if you buy a building or a property that can be split into separate dwellings and far increase the value compared to what it was worth as a single property. Investors either sell off the units or refinance to release the extra equity created. The way it usually works is to create structurally separate dwellings through refurbishing a property such as a house into flats just like medical student Will Gao did (featured in the case study in Chapter 2). If you want to sell these properties separately, they must also have their own separate supply of gas, electric and water (an extra cost to consider) as well as sound insulation and various other standards dictated by building regulations.

The new properties can either be sold as freehold or leasehold. The term *title splitting* arises from the process of creating leases for dwellings that were originally part of a freehold property. When a lease gets very short or is due to expire, the freeholder can charge a hefty premium to renew it, and can also charge ground rent. You will need a solicitor to draw up and create the leases.

TOP TIP

This is a complex area so make sure you speak to a commercial solicitor or lease specialist.

CHAPTER 6

MONEY, MONEY, MONEY—HOW TO FUND YOUR DEALS

The idea of not having enough (or indeed, any) money to invest in property is a common obstacle for most people starting out. It's also a common problem for big developers as, no matter how much personal cash or investor cash you have access to, there are only so many deals that can be done at one time. Therefore, it's time to overcome any negative thoughts you might have had about never being able to invest and realise that *everyone* runs out of cash at some point. Developers who have used up their own funds either wait for a project to complete to get their funds back out or find investment from elsewhere. Guess what most do? They find money from elsewhere which enables them to continue doing business and building new housing developments.

Broadly speaking, you can think of funding sources in terms of your own money and funds from other sources. Read through the different sources of funding below and write a list of any contacts you may know who might lend some money to you from each category. Don't forget that these sources of money could be used to fund the deposit or the rest of the purchase, the refurbishment, legal fees or any other property cost that comes up.

Personal savings

If you have personal savings, you may be in a position to invest in a property with or without mortgage finance. This may be through buying a property or controlling a property through strategies such as lease options or rent to rent.

Equity release

If you're already a homeowner and your property has gone up in value since purchase, you may be able to release equity through taking out a mortgage or re-mortgaging (rather than obtaining it by selling your property). In essence, you're borrowing money from the bank against the value of your home. Many people do this to fund another investment or home improvement such as an extension. You will need to assess the current market value of your property and speak to a mortgage broker about this so they can advise you (based on your personal situation) on whether the bank might approve the equity release. This will depend on your salary or annual income, your outgoings and how much equity you want to release. If the equity is being released from a rental property, the amount released will depend more on the rental income than your salary.

Using your pension to invest in property

It's also possible to invest in commercial property using a self-invested personal pension (SIPP). You should always take financial advice as there are specific criteria for investing in property using a pension, and you should certainly have educated yourself in property investment before taking any risks with your pension funds (or any other funds for that matter). However, many people have realised that the returns they can make from property (both in the short term in terms of cash flow, and in the long term considering capital growth) are far greater than the returns they can make from their pension. Depending on the type of investment strategy chosen this may require a degree of involvement in managing the properties (you can outsource this if you do not want to do it yourself), but for many people the advantages far outweigh those of a hands-free and low interest/gain pension.

Inheritance

You may be lucky enough to inherit funds or assets from a relative or from another source. If you're due an inheritance at a certain time, you can enquire whether your inheritance could be released to you early. Again, depending on the value of the inheritance and what strategy you choose, you could consider using inheritance funds to kick-start your property investment journey. It goes without saying that you must consider any inheritance tax due on the funds inherited, if applicable!

Family and friends

When entrepreneurs set out looking for seed funding to get their project or business to the next level, commonly the first source of funding they turn to is that belonging to family and friends. Make a list of your warm contacts (family, friends and close contacts) who might lend you money for your first project. Although some people might lend you this money out of the goodness of their hearts, and because they trust and believe in you, why not make it worthwhile for them and offer them a good rate of interest or a share of the profits in return for the loan? Note that the interest earned on loans is subject to income tax and the lender's personal income tax rate.

This source of funding isn't without its difficulties. Borrowing money from family and friends can cause tension and stress, and worse still ruin relationships (particularly if things go wrong), so consider this funding source carefully and make sure your deal is watertight! This should be done using a proper legal document (a loan agreement) which a solicitor can draw up for you and tailor to your needs. It's worth paying to do things right and ensure the terms you agree are clear to both yourself and the lender and there is no margin for misunderstanding.

Mortgage finance for doctors (and medical students!)

You may already be familiar with the concept of using mortgage finance to fund property purchases but if not here is a brief explanation. The buyer provides the deposit funds (typically anything between 5-50% of the purchase price) and the lender/bank provides the remainder, known as *mortgage finance* (in return for an agreed % interest per year). The vast majority of investors use mortgage finance to finance their investments as it is the best way to leverage their cash. Due to current low interest rates (2-5% for BTL), it's also a cheap way of financing deals without using up all your own cash. For example, if you use £100,000 cash to buy one house worth £100,000 your cash flow and capital appreciation are limited. If you use the same £100,000 to buy four £100,000 houses with a £25,000 mortgage on each, you can benefit from a greater cash flow and capital appreciation over a period of time.

Please note that mortgage interest rates and criteria are subject to change, so make sure you get the most up to date advice by using a mortgage broker. Below are some mortgage tips I gleaned from an interview with Lee Langley, founder of OnPoint Mortgages (www.onpointmortgages.com).

Guidance for doctors who are first-time buyers

If you are buying a property outright to live in, you could put down as little as 5% as a deposit, and also despite the August 2018 increase in the Bank of England Base rate, the cost of mortgages is still incredibly low. The amount of the loan will primarily be based on your income and expenditure, so it can be important to look at a provider or speak with a broker who understands your profession and how you're paid when looking to make the most of your budget. For example, some lenders can offer enhanced affordability calculations for professionals, such as doctors, that will enable you to borrow more than you would be able to otherwise. Another important point can be the way shift allowances, overtime and other additional payments over and above a basic salary are treated, with different lenders taking anywhere between 25% and 100% of these figures into account. Finally, for anyone working within the health industry who doesn't yet have the permanent right to reside in the UK, lending options are available; it comes down to the type of visa you have, the years remaining on the visa and your employment track record.

BTL Mortgages for FTB doctors

Options are reduced for first time buyers on a BTL basis as a lot of lenders pulled out of this market after the recession in 2008. A BTL loan is typically based on the expected rental income, rather than a customer's income and expenditure, so withdrawing from this type of lending was a way for banks to avoid someone borrowing a higher amount than they would otherwise be able to by using a BTL product, then living in the property themselves. More and more providers are moving back into this sector, however, and they are protecting themselves by assessing the application in two ways. Firstly, they calculate the loan using the usual BTL rental assessment, but they also base the lending on your personal income as well, as if you were going to live in the property. This is great news for the industry as we're seeing a trend of more and more first-time buyers choosing to invest in a buy to let so they can get onto the ladder and generate income from the property, while leaving them with the flexibility to rent in an ideal area, where they couldn't afford to buy otherwise.

Mortgages for locum doctors

A lender's approach varies depending on how you are set up. If you operate as a sole trader or via a limited company, they will usually want to see at least a year's accounts or personal tax returns. For a sole trader they would look at your net profit and for a limited company typically it is your salary and dividends. Alternatively, if you are paid directly on a PAYE basis or via an umbrella company, ensure you keep copies of any payslips and P60s to show a track record of regular work. The key is having clear proof of your income and satisfying the underwriter that the income is sustainable. Even if you have a limited track record as a locum, a specialist broker may be able to help depending on your personal circumstances and career history by using a more bespoke provider.

Doctors buying a second property as an investment

As well as the aforementioned different ways in which the loans are usually calculated, the deposit requirement is larger for BTL or HMO mortgages with the minimum amount being 15%, subject to the rental calculation fitting. Interest only borrowing is more readily available for BTL—great for those looking to keep the monthly payments down to generate a cash flow from the rent. For BTL mortgages, lenders will look at your credit history, source of your deposit and personal details even if purchasing the BTL within a limited company. One common misconception about HMOs is that you need to have a track record of letting properties previously but there are specialist lenders who can lend to first time landlords looking to buy a HMO as their first property investment. Deposit requirement in this instance, however, increases to a minimum of 20%.

Mortgages for medical students

If buying a property to live in, as the loan is based on income, the only way could be for a parent or parents to act as a guarantor or a joint applicant. Again, lenders can be more flexible in this scenario due to the job prospects after graduation. Initially, however, the parents will need to show they could afford the mortgage along with any other expenditure. You also need to be aware of any stamp duty implications on a joint application. Or if looking at a BTL property, for the first purchase at least, partnering up with someone who does own a property and has a regular income is an option. Be aware certain lenders can have a minimum age limit of twenty-one (sometimes even twenty-five) for BTL. Another option for those with a pot of funds can be investing in other people's projects, say via a regulated crowdfunding platform. Ensure you carry out your due diligence on the developer and what security they are offering to you.

Mortgages or GPs buying a practice premises

It can often be more beneficial to raise the funds against the practice itself, especially for younger doctors looking to buy a share but who have not yet built enough personal equity in their own homes. By lending to the practice, the bank has more security as it can secure its loan against the freehold and this typically means a better rate can be offered. For example, a high street lender like Barclays (who have a strong proposition in this field) will base the lend against the notional rent the practice receives from the NHS. This income provides a lot of comfort to lenders; it can be evidenced in the profit and loss accounts and allows them to be flexible. Using the example of Barclays, if the monthly payments of the requested loan will total £24,000 over a year, they will then require £24,000 of annual notional rent. A statement of assets, liabilities, income and expenditure (SALIE) will also be required for the directors and copies of the accounts are other important factors, especially if purchasing an existing practice. Valuation of the building is based on its bricks and mortar value and they can lend over a maximum twenty-year term, but anything over five years will be stress tested.

Bridging loans

Bridging finance can be a useful but expensive way to fund properties. Bridging finance is sometimes used by investors to complete on properties they want to refurbish and later refinance using a conventional mortgage to release the cash invested in the deal plus some profits. It is also used in a variety of emergency situations where there is a risk of losing a deal and cash is needed fast to complete the purchase. Some people use bridging finance at auctions; they might have paid a 10% deposit using their own cash but need to complete the purchase asap to get on with the refurbishment. Access to bridging finance is faster than applying for a mortgage and the endless paperwork that can entail. The main drawback with bridging finance is the high cost (typically 1% per month plus considerable entry/exit fees), so you need to do your due diligence on the deal to ensure the cost of finance is easily covered, including how any delays to your project could impact your ability to pay back the loan and the impact on your profit margins! However, while bridging is expensive compared to standard mortgages, the price is coming down thanks to increased competition in the market. Lee Langley told me that even bridging loan facilities at around 75% LTV (considered high) are being priced at around 0.75% per month with some cheaper deals available for lower LTVs and clients with experience of straightforward projects.

Joint venture finance

This funding source is similar to the above where you consider a joint venture (JV) with another investor who puts up the funds in return for your knowledge, time or other asset you bring to the deal. A joint venture involves sharing the risks as well as the rewards and should only be carried out with a high net worth or sophisticated investor in accordance with the Financial Conduct Authority's (FCA) guidance.[14] A reminder here that I am not FCA approved nor a financial advisor so please ensure that you get financial advice from a qualified person before proceeding with a JV. However, below is a brief summary of what I have found to be the most important points to consider when it comes to joint venture projects.

If you want to do a JV with someone then you will need to pre-qualify the individual to assess whether they are a high net worth individual or not. This process includes the self-certification of the individual who confirms whether they are a HNWI or other, identity checks, proof of funds and so on. It serves to protect those who may not be able to make an informed decision about financial investments and the risk involved. If someone does not meet the criteria to be classified as a HNWI then you may not be able to do a JV with them but instead offer them a fixed rate of interest on any funds loaned to you. Again, always take financial and legal advice.

If you want to do a joint venture with more than one person, then you must be FCA approved which means that you are approved to run financial promotions for collective investments (investment schemes involving more than one investor). If you are not FCA approved and you are conducting a financial promotion (be it having a conversation about a project, sharing documents, posting online etc) then it is considered to be a criminal act and you can be prosecuted. This is because you would be sharing something that you should be approved for prior.

I have had discussions countless times with people I do not know who approach me asking if they can do a JV or invest with me. Some of these people become irritated if I suggest we cover the basic formalities before discussing the details of any prospective projects. This is to protect them as well as myself and ensure that if we do a JV, that we structure it correctly. Too many times I've heard, 'But so-and-so has been offering/discussing deals with me without asking for all these documents,' which just demonstrates how many people do not conduct their business in a compliant manner.

Whether you are the person running the project or investing the funds, you should never feel pressured into investing in a deal or discussing investment opportunities without completing the basic compliance. If someone is not willing to do things properly from the very beginning, imagine what might happen later down the line. Finding the right business partner can take time and the process of getting into a financial relationship with someone should not be rushed. On the plus side, when JVs go right they can be hugely beneficial and help you to learn and achieve more by working with others than you could ever do by trying to do it all yourself. I have done several JVs myself and overall have had a very positive experience.

Peer to peer loans

In peer-to-peer lending, investors lend to people or businesses who repay the cash plus interest accrued over the term of the loan. This is desirable for investors who want to earn a good return on their cash that may otherwise be left sitting in the bank. There are now peer-to-peer lending platforms dedicated to arranging loans between investors and property developers for their property projects. One such platform is Blend Network which offers opportunities for lenders to invest anything from £1,000 upwards and earn up to 15% return per annum secured against property. (You can find out more at www.blendnetwork.com.).

Crowdfunding

Crowdfunding has burst onto the property scene in recent years with a variety of platforms available through which anyone can invest in property for a good return or raise funds for their projects. Like peer-to-peer lending, the great thing about these platforms is that they make it possible for anyone to invest as little as £50 in a deal and, provided that the project is successful, reap the rewards of investing in property 'hands-free'. It's possible to crowdfund the equity (where investors are shareholders in the business and can earn a percentage of the profits) or to crowdfund the debt part of the funding required (where investors generally earn a fixed return on the funds borrowed).

From the property developer's perspective, they get their deal analysed by the platform (which often requires a project to meet minimum criteria) and they can access a wider group of potential investors and ensure they are FCA compliant. The platform takes care of the legal side with regards to having multiple investors on board and ensures that they are eligible to invest. I have always wanted to find a way to help doctors to profit from property investments without requiring huge lump sums to get started. When I found out about crowdfunding, it seemed like the perfect way to help people like doctors get involved in projects normally only available to professional investors. In May

2018, I decided to offer the medical community the opportunity to co-invest with myself and my business partner doctor-developer John Friis in a commercial to residential conversion project—the Station Road Project in Sevenoaks, Kent. Below is a summary of our project finances.

Project costs

Purchase price	£437,500
Purchase costs	£56,550 (includes conveyancing, SDLT and professional fees)
Development cost	£373,054 (includes professional fees and interest on debt)
Selling cost	£16,600

Gross development value (GDV) of 6 flats £1,100,000

Profits

Gross profit	£216,296
Net profit	£165,007

Funding required for the project

Total equity investment	£240,000
Total debt required	£650,000

We aimed to raise £80,000 and offered our investors a projected return of 20% on their funds. The project was so popular that twenty-eight speedy investors over-funded it in just seven minutes, raising almost £93,000! We are converting a 2,700 ft^2 (250 m^2), commercial property (currently used as an office block), into six residential apartments which we will sell. We are really delighted to be sharing our process, skills and experience with our investors and hope that by learning while they earn, they can also develop the knowledge and confidence to do their own projects in the future. We funded our project through the Simple Crowdfunding platform and you can take a look at our Station Road crowdfunding project on the website below, and if interested, register your interest for our next project at https://www.simplecrowdfunding.co.uk/property/detail/1098.

The pitfalls of crowdfunding? For me there are very few. An important consideration is that most platforms will charge quite a high fee on the debt or equity raised, so you need to include this extra fee in your deal costs and analysis. If you are not able to raise the cash required, it can have a negative impact, as people may lose confidence in the developer or the project without good reason. If you end up not raising the cash required to complete the deal, it can create an assumption about the developer or the deal and potentially damage your reputation. Crowdfunding also looks easier than it is, and a crowdfunding campaign requires careful and timely planning.

CASE STUDY

Dr John Friis, property developer, Kent and former consultant anaesthetist, London

John has been a property investor since 2007. He rented out the flat he'd owned in Greenwich since 2004 until he sold it in 2009. Despite selling his property at the peak of the recession, his property had gone up in value by 35% over the previous five years. John realised two things at this point—property investing could generate great returns and he'd made a mistake in selling his property! He should have re-mortgaged it, withdrawn equity from the property and used that equity to invest in further investment properties. He subsequently went on to do exactly that and built up a portfolio of five investment properties in south London, which he rents out on either assured shorthand tenancies or as serviced apartments.

Until 2016, John had never considered leaving a career in anaesthesia. But he came to realise two things. One, that he had an idea, a vision of how he saw his life ten years in the future. He knew a career in anaesthesia was not going to help him realise what he wanted for his life. Two, he realised what was most important to him, what his highest values were; to be his own boss, to be in control of his life and to live life on his own terms.

John knew the reason he was so successful in anaesthesia was because he had incredible role models and mentors to help guide and shape his medical career. He decided to apply the same principles to learning more about property and once he learnt about the various property strategies and found mentors to help him on his journey, John never looked back.

John's first commercial property development was a joint-venture with one of his mentors. John invested his own money to help fund the acquisition of this development. It is a 33,000 $ft.^2$ (3065 m^2) office building in Bristol. This building will be converted to fifty-six apartments, a mixture of one bedroom and two-bedroom apartments under permitted development rights (formal planning permission isn't required to develop it). The development will have an estimated gross development value of £9.6 million.

Doing this JV gave John the confidence and the knowledge to take on his own developments such as the one aforementioned in Sevenoaks that he and I crowdfunded in May 2018. It's an office building that will be converted to 1-bedroom apartments with a gross development value of £1.2 million. It will be complete in July 2019. Together we have £200k in joint venture finance and £620k of debt finance to develop this project. In return for providing finance, our investors (all twenty-eight of them!) get an excellent return on their money. Moreover, they will also learn along the way how to develop property themselves should they so choose to do so in the future.

John now has what he wanted, to live life on his own terms. He has time to spend with his young family. His business is growing. He works with a number of joint venture investors who realise the benefits of working in partnership with a developer i.e. that both sides win in such a symbiotic relationship. John continues to be on the lookout for more investor partners, particularly among his ex-colleagues. He's a passionate exponent of empowering his fellow medics to open their eyes and realise the possibilities that life brings their way.

CHAPTER 7

REFURBS AND DEVELOPMENTS

So why refurbish your property? Refurbishment and renovation can add a lot of value to a property you want to rent, sell or release equity from. It can make all the difference when it comes to getting a great price for your property as fast as possible and is often an easy way to beat the competition. Refurbishment need not be an expensive process and I've included as many tips and tricks as possible below to help you out! However, it's always important to evaluate the cost-benefit of carrying out a refurbishment due to the time and financial investment involved.

Refurbishing your first property can be a daunting task, particularly if you have no experience. I felt nervous the first time I did a refurb on a studio flat in London. There were so many decisions to make and I was worried my lack of experience would result in me being ripped off by tradespeople or I would make the wrong decisions about materials, layouts and a whole host of things. The truth is I did make a few mistakes—everyone does, but I hope that you can avoid making the same mistakes I did by using the guidance in this chapter.

The terms *refurbishment* or *renovation* are used to cover a whole host of changes you can make to a property, ranging from giving a property a lick of paint to carrying out a full refurbishment where the property is gutted, everything is replaced, maybe including minor structural alterations such as moving walls.

Cosmetic refurbishment

Some property projects require little work to bring them up to a desirable market standard and may only require simple changes such as painting and decorating, changing soft furnishings such as carpets and blinds, or renewing and replacing items that have started to look tired (for example, re-grouting tiles, re-sealing bath tubs with silicone or replacing small items such as kitchen worktops or wall tiles).

Staging

You may want to consider staging a property for sale or to let. This generally entails partly or fully furnishing a property with small details to make it look more desirable and to give the end user an idea of what living there may look or feel like. It's also used to illustrate or sell a particular lifestyle to the target end user. You can either buy the furnishings yourself, rent the furniture or instruct a staging company to do it for you. I had a friend who used to part-stage her rental properties using the same formula which consisted of a beautiful chandelier; grey carpets; a sofa and coffee table in the lounge; a few candles here and there and a fresh bunch of flowers in a vase. Below is a list of items you may want to use to stage your property (by room type). By no means do you need to get all items nor spend a lot of money; the idea is to show someone the property looking its best and most desirable. Staging my properties has always paid off and creates a great impression from the start.

Lounge: Sofa; coffee table or nest tables; rug; candles; vase of flowers; a couple of framed prints to hang on a wall; a magazine or coffee table book; floor lamp; ceiling chandelier or decent lampshade; curtains or blinds.

Kitchen: Dining table and chairs with cutlery; glasses; plates; napkins laid out for two to four people; vase and flowers or artificial potted plants; one or two framed prints for the walls; coffee machine; a nice bowl of fresh lemons, limes or oranges.

Bathroom: A couple of fluffy white towels laid out or rolled up in a basket hotel style; posh hand gel and hand lotion; a small plant.

Bedroom: A double bed dressed in linen (for example, duvet, pillows, scatter cushions and pretty throw); rug; an accent chair; bedside tables; bedside lamps; one or two framed prints for the walls; two or three candles or small ornaments for bedside table; bed linen.

Small renovations

You may carry out small renovations in the property such as replacing some or all of the bathroom fixtures and fittings or installing a new kitchen.

Complete refurbishment

Properties that are completely outdated or uninhabitable may require *complete refurbishment.* This generally means gutting/demolition of kitchens and bathrooms; re-plastering walls; replacing flooring; replacing electrical wiring and fuse box; renewing plumbing; repairing or replacing the roof and so on.

Structural changes

Refurbishing a property can often significantly increase its value. Apart from increasing its value by making it look nice you can increase the value by creating more space or a more desirable layout. For example, an increasingly popular strategy with property developers is to eliminate hallways (sometimes considered a waste of space) to design brighter and more spacious homes. When it comes to increasing the size of the property, there are a number of ways to do this (for example, by converting a loft into an extra room or extending to the side or to the back of the property).

Building and development

Building and developments are the most ambitious property projects as they entail building a property from scratch or converting a building from one use class into another (for example, a commercial to residential property). This isn't for the faint hearted and requires a lot of experience (or a lot of courage and great contacts!). To carry out a property development you need to ensure you have professionals such as a planning consultant, architect, quantity surveyor, broker for development finance, building contractor and many more involved.

Where do I find a good builder?

This is a common question. While below I use the term 'builder' and assume all the work will be carried out by the same team, bear in mind that you may want to run the project yourself and subcontract out elements of work (for example, plumbing, electrics or painting and decorating). This can work out cheaper but is more time consuming.

Word of mouth recommendations

First, reach out to your network of trusted friends and family for recommendations. You need to ask who they used and how long ago the work was carried out. Did the refurb project run to time and cost? Who sourced the materials (them or the builder and, if it was the builder, did they give the builder clear instructions on style and quality)? Can they show you photos or take you to see the work? Did anything go wrong and if so how did they solve the problem? Would they be happy to use the same builder again?

Online marketplaces for builders

If you can't get a decent recommendation from someone in your network, rather than turn to Google you could use an online marketplace to find tradespeople and read reviews from their previous clients. One that comes to mind is Ratedpeople.com where you can post a job description, budget and timeframe and get three requests to quote within forty-eight hours. Other options are Checkatrade.com and Mybuilder.com. Some tips:

1. The more detailed your description the better.
2. Provide photos of the job you are posting about, if you can.
3. Be aware that if you need a job done urgently you may end up with a 'desperate builder'—most good builders aren't readily available due to being busy on jobs though this is not always the case.
4. Never post your maximum budget as most builders will work to the budget you post regardless of how much work/materials cost.

5. The due diligence you can do on builders listed on these websites is often inadequate.

I have found highly skilled but also awful builders via these platforms in the past. Just like finding any other competent professional, finding a good builder is sometimes a matter of trial and error. Keep in mind that even when you find a good one the results will depend on the skills of their team members.

How to know when you're looking at good quality work

Knowing whether a builder's work is 'good' or not is tough in the beginning. It's like asking a non-medic to comment on whether a doctor has treated the patient correctly or not. Luckily, there are a few ways to deal with this problem. Firstly, you could take someone with more experience with you to look at the previous work of the builder and explain to you what they're assessing (in person). Don't just look at photos as they can hide a whole host of problems and errors. It's far better to view the work in person. Secondly, you can ask the person who instructed the builder whether they have had any problems or noticed any issues with the work. For example, it isn't until you use a bath or shower that you can tell whether there are any leaks or whether the bath has been fitted correctly (there should be no pooling of water on the lip/edges of the bath when the shower is running which would indicate the feet have not been fitted correctly—and yes, unfortunately this happened to me!) Look carefully at tiling to check if all tiles are lined up and there is equal space/grouting between the tiles.

There are plenty of videos on YouTube and resources on the internet you can find to help you check the quality of building work. I'm no expert and had to learn through some painful mistakes as well as common sense (for example, checking the gap between wall tiles is homogenous throughout or newly plastered walls are perfectly smooth and flat or kitchen wall units are hung correctly—I soon got used to using a spirit level to check work like this!). It's difficult to ascertain the quality of someone's work when you don't have experience in the field. Your best bet is to get references from previous clients followed by assessing in person. If the work gives you the wow factor, go with your gut feeling. Otherwise, assess as suggested above by checking the aesthetic quality of the work. Furthermore, if you have a good project manager for the refurb you can often avoid costly mistakes and poor workmanship, but you obviously need to work this into your price and budget.

How much will my refurbishment cost?

The cost of a project will vary depending on cost of materials, cost of labour in your part of the country and any extra considerations such as supply and removal of a skip, parking costs, and any professional fees (for example, planning and architects' services). Always get three estimates and give all three builders the same brief, asking them to itemise the quotation for each item listed, and ask them if you have missed anything that needs to be included. This way you can compare the quotes easily and query any areas where there is a big discrepancy in price.

You tend to get three types of builder: cheap guys who usually underestimate time and cost of the job, expensive builders who people assume may be better quality but they often subcontract the work to another company and make a profit on the margin, and finally the middle guys who charge an appropriate price and do things in-house. You can always ask your builder whether they subcontract parts of the job and, if so, to whom.

You also need to decide on the level of specification your target market will be expecting, and how important this is. For example, in a student property you would aim for a hard-wearing laminate kitchen worktop whereas for a property aimed at an owner occupier or high-end lettings market you may want to go for a granite worktop. For other items there is little difference in appearance between an acrylic bath that costs £100 and one that costs £300, so consider durability and ask around for advice.

Should you or your builder source materials?

Most builders will offer you the option of sourcing materials for you at cheaper prices than you might be able to access. There a couple of things to consider here:

1. Builders can source and supply basic building materials *and* fixtures and fittings or a mixture. I usually get mine to source the basic building materials and I choose the fixtures and fittings, including tiles and wall paint colours. You can negotiate about who will be responsible for ordering the items.

2. Your builder's taste may not be the same as yours (or appropriate for the market you're targeting) so if you want your builder to source something for you (and the type or style of materials matters to you), give them as detailed a brief as possible or ask to see pictures of the items they're buying before they purchase.

3. Builders who have business accounts with suppliers often get materials at trade prices. Some kind builders will pass this discount directly on to their client, while others charge a small fee for sourcing on top. Sourcing, ordering and collecting materials can be time consuming so I don't mind the builder making some money on materials as it saves me time and makes it worthwhile for them. However, if you want to save money, opening a trade account for your property investment business and doing the sourcing and ordering yourself can really pay off!

How to get great discounts on materials, fixtures and fittings

If you have or are starting a legitimate property business, you can register for a trade account at most building merchants and kitchen or joinery stores (for example, Travis Perkins, Lawsons, Screwfix or Magnet). You can get a lot of great materials online these days. Using eBay and other websites can be a great way to source expensive brands for a fraction of the usual price. I have done this several times for good quality bathroom and kitchen taps.

Many property investor or landlord organisations and clubs are able to negotiate great member discounts with companies. One I suggest you look at joining is the Landlords National Property Group (LNPG) who can get some incredible discounts on kitchens, bathrooms, boilers, electrics and other items. You pay an annual membership fee but can save thousands on your refurbishments. Another organisation that can get you good discounts is the National Landlord Association (NLA).

Is my builder legitimate?

There are too many horror stories when it comes to people being scammed by rogue builders. I suppose, much like in healthcare, it can be difficult to decipher the type and legitimacy of the qualifications of an industry you're unfamiliar with. One way to do this is to ask your builder for the following:

1. Any professional qualifications or registrations and where you can cross check the information. N.B. Electricians and gas engineers have separate regulatory bodies much like the General Medical Council.[15] You can check whether a tradesman is certified in the same way you check whether a doctor holds a licence to practice online.

2. Indemnity insurance certificate including details of the policy and the insurer.

3. If they have their own company, their company records on Companies House online.

4. Recommendations and references from previous clients.

Ensuring the project runs to time and cost

The best way to avoid issues throughout the duration of the project is to draw up a basic contract with agreed schedule of works including timescales, roles and responsibilities of everyone involved, and

15 Electricians may be registered with the National Inspection Council for Electrical Contracting (NICEIC) or ELECSA and gas engineers may be listed on the Gas Safety Register.

contingency planning for unexpected events or extra work that may come up (or be requested by you). The more detailed you can be, the better. Make sure you factor in time required to source and order materials (there can often be a lead time of three to four weeks for items such as kitchens, and popular fixtures and fittings can sometimes go out of stock). My father helped me write my first contract and schedule of works and, being an engineer, he is very detail oriented, so I still use this for small projects to this day! However, you can find a number of template contracts online or ask your property solicitor to draw one up for you. You may want to consider a financial reward for projects that run to time or finish early and financial penalties for a project that runs late without reason (for example, unexpected problems that arise or delays with materials).

Sofoclis Patsalosavvis, from construction company Seventeen Build, suggests using a simple contract from the Joint Contracts Tribunal (JCT)[16] who produce standard forms of contract for homeowners and tradespeople in the construction industry. In addition, you should always check that the builder's insurance covers both public liability and the cost/value of the project. For bigger projects (for example, building or significant conversion work), you can get a quantity surveyor (QS) to provide a detailed breakdown of a project's cost and schedule and administer a contract based on this. Quantity surveyors go into painstaking detail and they have insurance to back them up and they can save your neck from things going pear-shaped. They also rigorously review any contractors bidding for the tender on your project and can be a good buffer against selecting a contractor who is about to go bust.

Having a contract is a great way to protect yourself from things going wrong. However, if things do go wrong and you're unable to solve a dispute yourself, there are people you can hire to assist in the dispute resolution process who you can find through the Royal Institute of

16 You can browse the JCT's resources here: JCT, *JCT Online Store*, https://www.jctltd.co.uk/ [accessed 13 November 2018].

Chartered Surveyors' (RICS) website.[17]

Sofoclis gave me his tips from the builder's viewpoint on how to prevent running over cost and budget. He advised that it's important to be realistic about the budget and time required to complete a project and most people don't build a big enough contingency into their refurb budgets. Unexpected costs or changes almost always come up as you never know what lies beneath the structure you are about to knock down or rip out. He also advised to start planning a project as early as possible as special fixtures can take a long time to order as the big decisions to be made around interiors!

For those of you applying for planning permission he advises speaking to a builder *before* you apply for planning as it's always better to start the conversation early and benefit from the insights and experience of your builder prior to submitting any plans. Again, employing a project manager to ensure your project runs to time and budget can be a big advantage if you're short of time. Sure, it will incur extra costs, but the alternative is for you to be prepared to spend a lot of time on the project, call and meet with each tradesperson, order materials, receive and check them on site and review quotations (and understand them). It's a great learning experience but may not be worth your time.

Design tips

People either love or hate the interior design stage. Those who love it relish in creating a particular look and choosing colour schemes and materials to match. Others find this process overwhelming and stressful due to the number of possibilities and decisions to be made. You often stumble upon a formula that works and end up sticking to it. At one point my formula was grey walls, Scandinavian-style wood flooring and a lovely chandelier.

You can have different formulas depending on the market you're targeting. For example, in the lettings market you may have formulas

17 You can browse dispute resolution services here: Royal Institute of Chartered Surveyors, *RICS Dispute Resolution Service*, https://www.rics.org/uk/footer/dispute-resolution-service/ [accessed 13 November 2018].

to attract students, young professionals, mature professionals, couples, families and so on. The interior design is your opportunity to make your property shine and stand out, so if you don't enjoy this part please don't paint the whole house beige or magnolia—make sure you find someone to help you! I have seen some student HMOs that are more beautiful and stylish than family homes on the market (and at low cost too!). Creating a mood board using a website like Pinterest or getting ideas from interior design magazines can help you plan and decide on what look you are going for as well as give you new ideas on how to cheaply stage a property! Remember you don't need to re-invent the wheel. Find a look you like and replicate it.

TOP TIPS

Consider the target market you are renting or selling to and not what you would want to see in your own home.

Always get three quotations from different contractors and add on 20% contingency costs.

Get word of mouth recommendations for a builder where possible or ask for previous references and ideally proof of previous projects.

Check the indemnity and insurance costs of the builder and ensure they cover your project.

Consider staging or part-staging your property to get more interest and faster conversions.

Use contracts to protect yourself in the event that things go wrong.

CHAPTER 8

PROPERTY TAX TIPS FOR DOCTORS BY SIMON MISIEWICZ, OPTIMISE TAX ACCOUNTANTS

There is little point in earning good money only to lose it all in taxes because of poor planning or record keeping. The information provided below is based on the tax rates for 2017/18 and 2018/19. There are elements of tax points for 2019/20 and 2020/21 for Section 24 mortgage interest relief cap on residential property investments. The information shared in this chapter does not constitute tax advice and you ought to seek tax advice that takes into account your personal circumstances.

Fail to plan and you'll plan to fail

Good record keeping is essential for any entrepreneur. Bookkeeping and admin are important facets of your business and can lead to success if done correctly—or ruin if neglected.

Every person, company and organisation in the land wishes to reduce tax. But it's one thing to want to make things happen and quite another to have the right level of knowledge to execute a tax-efficient plan.

There have been major tax changes of late with the introduction of increased Stamp Duty Land Tax (SDLT) of 3% on top of the usual SDLT banded charges. Anyone who wishes to buy a residential investment property in their own name but already has a property (whether an investment property or their own home) will need to pay the additional 3% SDLT surcharge. Anyone wanting to buy a residential investment property in a limited company will also need to pay the 3% SDLT surcharge.

Next came another change called Section 24. Due to this, by the 2020/2021 tax year the amount of mortgage interest you will be able to offset against your property income will be reduced to nil.

From 2020/21 your property tax will be calculated based on the rental income and running costs of the property, not considering the mortgage interest. You will instead get a 20% tax reducer of the lower of:

a) mortgage interest

b) property profits or

c) total taxable income

It might be helpful to know that pre 2017/18, property investors were allowed to offset 100% of their mortgage costs against their property income. From 2017/18 the amount of mortgage interest allowed to be offset against property income will be reduced to 75%. There will be a further reduction of 25% each year until 2020/21 when no allowance will be made to offset mortgage interest against property income in order to calculate tax due.

In place of mortgage interest being a tax deductible cost will be a 20% tax reducer. This tax reducer is calculated as 20% of the lower of:

Mortgage interest costs

Property profit (excluding mortgage interest as a cost)

Taxable income as a whole

The tax reducer will start at 25% for the tax year 2017/18. This will increase by 25% until 2020/21 when the 20% tax reducer will be set at 100% of the above values.

As you can see, HMRC are replacing the mortgage interest cost allowance with the mortgage tax reducer. For example, John is an employee earning £50,000 and had the following income/costs for property in 2016/17.

£50,000 rental income

£20,000 mortgage interest cost

£30,000 property profit

£12,000 buy to let tax liability (as a high rate tax payer paying 40% tax = £30,000 x 40%)

In 2017/18 the situation will be:

£50,000 rental income

£15,000 mortgage interest cost (reduced from £20,000)

£35,000 profit

£14,000 buy to let tax liability (as a high rate tax payer paying 40% tax = £35,000 x 40%)

However, the £14,000 is reduced by the tax reducer as follows:

25% of the 20% tax reducer rate is 5%. The 5% tax reducer rate is the lower of:

£35,000 property profit

£15,000 mortgage interest

£85,000 taxable income

Therefore, John receives a tax reducer of £750 (£15,000 X 5%). His tax liability is:

£14,000 tax calculated as above, minus £750 tax reducer leaves £13,250 tax to pay

John pays £1,250 more tax in 2017/18 than he did in the previous year on the same amount of profit.

The majority of our clients now use limited companies for their property investments. Not just because of the tax advantages but also the additional benefits we will look at later.

Tax planning

When thinking about tax planning, it's tempting to listen to friends or find out more from a website or social media channel. The problem is that generic advice isn't tailored towards your personal circumstances.

With tax planning, it's vital to think of the long term. You may need to consider the following scenarios:

- Career progression within the NHS and higher salary expectations
- Leaving the NHS and becoming a self-employed locum
- Becoming a consultant and starting a medical professional services business
- Leaving the medical profession and replacing your hard-earned money with rental profits

Your plans are for the future will have a direct impact on the amount of tax you will pay and how you structure your property investment business.

If you plan to be a high rate tax payer for the foreseeable future, it would be beneficial to invest in property using a limited company. If you're currently a high rate tax payer but your plans mean you're likely to become a basic rate tax payer, it may be more beneficial to buy some properties in your own name first.

There are other reasons why people use limited companies other than just tax planning. One advantage of using a limited company is that the risk remains within the limited company. People buying and holding single properties may not be much at risk of something going wrong. However, someone who deals with large property developments such as the building and construction of twenty flats, as an individual owner, will have a lot more risk involved compared to the risk and liability of something going wrong if they run the project using a limited company.

Tax planning can become complicated when:

a) Your circumstances change

b) Tax legislation also changes meaning the plans you have to save tax may make sense now but not so much tomorrow

That is why Optimise Accountants suggest that doctors and property investors should sit down with a tax specialist to discuss their plans. This is to ensure they put in place the right tax structure, which will remain applicable for the long term.

You could also speak with an accountant, but please bear in mind that while the role of tax advisors and accountants can appear similar, their knowledge, qualifications and skills can vary greatly. Just as in medicine where orthopaedic surgeons may specialise in different parts of the body, for example, hand or knee, you would not seek the advice of a knee surgeon for a problem with your hands. It really is worth the time and effort to speak with a tax qualified advisor when discussing your future investment plans to ensure that you invest in a way that makes sense for your personal situation.

Record keeping

If you fail to keep records two things will happen. Firstly, you will make far less profit than you anticipated because you didn't keep track of loss of rental income or control your costs. Secondly, if you don't keep clear and accurate records and HMRC investigate, you'll find it difficult to justify your tax calculations. You may then be liable for additional tax estimated by HMRC on your behalf.

You need to keep your receipts and any paper records for both income and costs for at least six years. This is the number of years HMRC can go back to investigate your tax affairs.

Keep your self-assessment tax return with supporting paper work together. Use an accountant to help you pull the numbers together so you have an independent and objective person checking the details.

Allowable expenses

When you own rental property, there are a number of expenses that are allowable deductions for tax purposes. However, there is a difference between running costs (which can be offset against your yearly income) and capital costs (which can only be offset against capital gain when you eventually sell the property).

It's important to be clear about the distinction at an early stage so you don't allocate costs incorrectly. You should keep all receipts, and preferably record their details on a spreadsheet or accounting software system, so when the time comes to offset them, you have the right evidence.

Capital expenses (allowed when the property is sold)

- Conveyancing fees for the purchase
- Finder's fees
- Stamp duty
- Surveys
- Improvements such as extensions
- *Revenue expenses (to offset against your property income)*
- Repairs such as exterior and interior painting, damp treatment, stone cleaning, roof repairs, furniture repairs
- Mortgage arrangement costs
- Legal fees associated with the loan (including legal fees related to mortgage financing of the property)
- Mortgage interest costs (bearing in mind mortgage interest relief changes)
- Insurance
- Agents' management fees
- Advertising costs

Getting the tax right on your refurbishment projects

If you build a loft extension, you're improving a property, so this is a capital expense. You can't offset it against your income, but you can offset it against any capital gain when you sell the property.

However, if you replace a tired kitchen with one of a similar size and style, this is a revenue expense and can be offset against any property income. If you carry out substantial repairs and make a loss on a property, this can be offset against any other property income you have for that year or offset the loss against property profits in future.

The specific types of refurbishment costs that may be offset against your income are:

- Repairs: carrying out repairs to broken units, roof tiles, furniture or plasterwork
- Renewals: repainting your property, cleaning costs
- Replacement: kitchen units, bathroom units, heating systems (boilers and radiators), lighting systems (including fuse boxes), carpets, curtains, fridges, freezers, TVs, beds, furniture (if all were in place at the time of purchase)

If you want to play it extra safe, you could ask the sellers of any property you're buying to itemise the following on the sales completion documents:

- Value of the land and building
- Value of the kitchen
- Value of bathrooms
- Value of white goods (if supplied as a rental)

This can be used as evidence that there were assets in the property at purchase and will support the fact that you're replacing or repairing those assets, meaning they can justifiably be offset against your property income.

Don't put the cost of a kitchen as costing £3,000 against your property income if the value in the sales documents only shows £1,000. The new kitchen will be seen as an improvement and will be considered a capital expense.

If you buy properties that are in a lettable state but are very tired, you can justify to HMRC that the refurbishment costs will help you to increase the rental income of the property. You can prove that the property is in a lettable state if you have a buy-to-let (BTL) mortgage which has a condition that the property must be in a lettable state within the application process.

Types of property

You need to make a decision about what type of property to invest in and where to invest. Sometimes the two will go hand in hand. For example, if you want to set up a shared house for students, you'll need to choose an area close to a university.

Residential property investing: single lets and HMOs

If you already have a business or employment that is generating enough money for your lifestyle, a single let may be the best strategy for you, particularly if it's capital growth you're looking for and you want less involvement with the running of the property.

You are likely to earn less ROI on a single let property than you are with a HMO, but you need to take into account the amount of time you put into your investment. Generally speaking, the average gross yield of a HMO can be double or even triple that of a single let.

Financing HMOs can also be tricky and costly if you're a first-time property investor, but there are more options available to those with experience of investing in single let properties.

Remember that residential property investment will be subject to the Section 24 mortgage interest relief cap.

Commercial

Commercial property includes shops, offices and restaurants, as well as holiday lets.

Although commercial property hasn't been the traditional first port of call for property investors, it has been drawing more attention since the announcement of the Section 24 mortgage interest relief cap. This is because commercial property is taxed differently to residential property. Loans secured against a commercial property continue to attract full interest relief. The 3% stamp duty surcharge discussed in the first section doesn't apply to commercial properties.

Another advantage of commercial property investment is that you can invest in commercial property via a self-invested personal pension (SIPP), which attracts tax relief at the highest tax band on most of the contributions you make.

Usually, when investing in residential property you'll be doing so using money you've already paid tax on. If you invest using a SIPP, you can invest using pre-tax income, which immediately boosts your ROI considerably. In addition, income and capital growth earned in a SIPP is tax-free.

Holiday lets

Holiday lets have attracted a lot of interest lately from investors who have historically invested primarily in residential property. Holiday lets are properties that would otherwise be standard residential accommodation but come with the tax advantages of commercial property. Therefore, Section 24 doesn't come into play and 100% of the mortgage interest cost can be offset against its income.

Investing in a holiday let could allow you to enjoy the same opportunity for growth as a standard buy-to-let, but without having to worry about whether or not to invest personally or via a limited company because of the tax changes.

Holiday lets are more time-consuming to manage than single lets, but there are many good holiday letting agencies that can take care of management for you.

Holiday lets/serviced accommodation must meet the conditions set in HMRC's *Help Sheet 253*:

- Your property must be available for letting as furnished holiday accommodation letting for at least 210 days in the year. Don't count any days when you're staying in the property. HMRC don't consider the property to be available for letting while you're staying there.
- You must let the property commercially as furnished holiday accommodation to the public for at least 105 days in the year (70 days for the tax year 2011 to 2012 and earlier). Don't count any days when you let the property to friends or relatives at zero or reduced rates as this isn't a commercial let. Don't count longer-term lets of more than 31 days, unless the 31 days is exceeded because something unforeseen happens.

For holiday lets, capital allowances include: Plant and machinery capital allowances for items such as furniture, equipment, fixtures, writing, plumbing and heating installation equipment.

The first £200,000 of a capital allowance may be claimed in any one tax year at 100%, provided that the capital allowances are claimed within year of purchase. If capital allowances are claimed after one year, the benefit is reduced from 100% to 8/18% depending on the type of asset claimed.

If the capital allowances create a loss, and the property is in your personal name, the loss may be offset against your other income from (for example) employment or self-employment. This may reduce your income tax liability.

All profits from your holiday let count as earnings for pension purposes (rather than being restricted to £3,600 maximum pension contributions if property investment is the only income received).

Please note that this type of income is subject to VAT, so if you have a turnover of £85,000 or more in any twelve-month rolling period you will need to register and charge VAT at 20%. Once you have registered, you can claim back any VAT suppliers charge you.

Section 24—mortgage interest relief cap

Back in the good old days, property investors were able to offset the mortgage interest they incurred on their residential property investment against their rental income. However, one of George Osborne's parting gifts was the introduction of Section 24, which is being phased in between 2017/18 to 2020/21.

In 2016/17 you were able to offset 100% of the residential mortgage interest against your property income.

In 2017/18 you were only able to offset 75% of the mortgage interest against your property income.

In 2018/19 you will only be able to offset 50% of the mortgage interest against your property income.

This 25% phased reduction to allow mortgage interest to be offset against your taxable income completes in 2020/21. This means you won't be able to offset any interest of your mortgage from that point. You will, however, receive a 20% tax reducer of mortgage interest against the tax liability of the property income. For high rate tax payers, this means you technically get 20% less tax relief against the mortgage interest, and additional rate tax payers receive 25% less tax relief.

Section 24 only affects residential property investments. It's worth considering investing in holiday lets, serviced accommodation, commercial property or car parks (for example) if you wish to avoid Section 24 but still wish to invest in property.

The UK's base rate has been at 0.5% or below for many years but interest rates may increase in the future. There is a compounding issue with Section 24 and the future increases to mortgage interest rates.

The amount of tax relief on mortgage interest is being withdrawn whilst the rate of interest increases.

As stated previously, Section 24 is being phased in. It's important to see how these changes will affect high rate tax payers. There is a misconception that basic rate tax payers will avoid the impact of Section 24. Sadly, this isn't true. HMRC consider that the mortgage interest you pay on your property portfolio will be treated as zero cost.

Section 24 impact: basic rate tax payers become high rate tax payers example:

	2015/16	2020/21
Employment income (1)	£20,000	£20,000
Rental income	£50,000	£50,000
Mortgage costs	£35,000	£0
Other costs	£5,000	£5,000
Property profit (2)	£10,000	£45,000
Taxable income (1) + (2)	£30,000	£65,000

This person has moved from being a basic rate tax payer to being a high rate tax payer from 2020/21 because of the mortgage interest relief cap. This means the top rate of tax they will pay becomes 40% rather than the 20% before the tax changes.

Section 24 impact: loss of personal allowance example

	2015/16	2020/21
Employment income (1)	£85,000	£85,000

Rental income	£50,000	£50,000
Mortgage costs	£35,000	£0
Other costs	£5,000	£5,000
Property profit (2)	£10,000	£45,000
Taxable income (1) + (2)	£95,000	£130,000

The person above has a taxable income of £95,000. However, once Section 24 is fully implemented their taxable income will be restated as £130,000. This means that they will lose their personal allowance of £11,850 (2018/19).

If you earn more than £100,000, your personal allowances will be eroded by £1 for every £2 of earnings above £100,000. For example, someone who earns £120,000 would lose an element of their personal allowance as follows (at today's rates, where the tax free personal allowance is £11,500):

Excess of earnings limit = £20,000 (£120,000 earnings less the £100,000 limit)

Reduction to personal allowance = £10,000 (£20,000 excess divided by 2)

Therefore, the revised personal allowance = £1,500 (£11,500 less £10,000)

Section 24 impact: loss of pension allowance

In the above example, earnings have increased from £95,000 to £130,000. This also means that the person above will start to lose the pension contributions allowance. You usually pay tax if savings in your pension pot go above your annual allowance. (This is currently £40,000 a year, provided you earned this amount of money.) From

April 2016 you'll have a reduced (tapered) annual allowance if both of the following apply:

- Your *threshold income* is over £110,000—this is your income excluding any pension contributions (unless they're paid as a salary sacrifice by your employer).
- Your *adjusted income* is over £150,000—this is your total taxable income after deductions have been made for tax reliefs (such as trading losses, charity donations, pension contributions etc) and before any personal allowances are accounted for.

For every £2 over the above-mentioned amounts you'll will see a reduction of £1 to your pension contribution allowance.

You can see from the above that the tax rate could be more than 40% because of Section 24. It therefore makes sense to invest in a limited company and extract this money only when you need it. If you decide to reinvest profits made within your limited company, it will be taxed at the current rate of 19%, which will be reduced to 17% in the future. This is a lot less than the 65% tax we have forecasted for some of our clients who hold property investments in their own name.

Limited companies

Should a doctor buy a property in their own name or in a limited company? This depends on their individual position and what plans they have for the future.

If your aim is to remain a high rate tax payer for many years because of your career plans, because you have other income or because Section 24 means you will be deemed a high rate tax payer, it may be worth buying property investments within a limited company. (Make sure you take appropriate tax advice before making any long-term decisions.)

There is an exception to the above rule. If you're married or have a civil partner who is a basic rate tax payer or pays no tax at all, it is worth considering buying a property in your joint names with the majority of income going to the lower tax earner rather than using a limited company.

The main advantage of using a limited company is that corporate tax rates (19%) are lower than income tax rates for basic rate tax payers (20%), high rate tax payers (40%) and additional rate tax payers (45%). The downside to using a limited company for property investing is that mortgage interest rates are typically higher than they would be in your personal name. You therefore need to weigh up the tax savings to the additional mortgage interest charges.

You also need to consider the additional administration of using a limited company and the additional accountancy fees of submitting accounts to Companies House and corporate tax schedules to HMRC.

You can get money out of a limited company by the following means:

Salary

If you don't receive any other form of wages from elsewhere and are not already a high rate tax payer (earning more than £46,350 in the 2018/19 tax year), you can take £8,424 (2018/19 tax year). You will now need to run a payroll system and notify HMRC that you're an employer (even if you're not paying tax or national insurance) if you take more than £116 per week (2018/19) or its equivalent.

Dividends

Dividends can only be paid out of post-tax retained profits. Therefore, if your business has made a loss rather than profit in a year and has no retained earnings, no dividends may be taken.

The first £2,000 dividends are tax free irrespective of how much money you earn (for the 2018/19 tax year and beyond). Any dividends in excess of £2,000 will be taxed as long as you remain a basic rate tax payer (when you add together dividends and salary and any other income landing in your personal name) at 7.5% (a basic rate tax payer is an individual whose total income is no greater than £46,350 in 18/19 tax year). If you take dividends in excess of £2,000 and are a high rate tax payer, you will pay 32.5% dividend tax (or

38.1% dividend tax as an additional rate tax payer).

If you wish to release interim dividends to the shareholders to take full advantage of dividend allowance in a particular tax year you will need to make the money transaction (move money from the limited company to the directors' personal bank accounts) and prepare an interim dividend certificate for each director receiving the dividend that shows the name of the company, value of dividend, which shareholders receive it and the date. You will also need to sign it as a director of the company. Keep a copy of all such documents so your accountant can ensure correct accounting treatment when your annual accounts are prepared. Remember, you can only pay a dividend at an interim date if at that date your accounts showed your business to be in profit.

Pension contributions

Your company can contribute towards its directors'/employees' pension. You can have a personal pension scheme, which may then invest in commercial properties. Any money the company pays into a pension is a cost and therefore reduces the profit of the business (is tax deductible).

Loans from directors

Any money the directors/employees have invested by way of loans to the limited company may also be taken out of the company tax free.

Key person insurance

Your company may also pay life assurance as keyman insurance that pays out a lump sum to a beneficiary/trust. This is not a benefit in kind for the employee. Paying money into a trust will avoid the painful IHT liability on your death. Any life insurance paid to your estate directly will have to pay the 40% IHT liability as it increases your net wealth.

Medical care

Employers can pay up to £500 medical bills on the behalf of their employees to get them back to work if they have been sick for at least 28 consecutive days. Employers can also pay for periodic medical checks or health screening each year without this becoming a benefit in kind. The company can also pay for eye tests (including glasses and contact lenses if used for VDU work).

Loans

Employees (not directors) may be provided with loans up to £10,000, and provided the employee pays back the loan with an interest rate at the official HMRC rate (currently 3.25%), there will not be a benefit in kind for the employee. However, a benefit in kind would arise if a company was to give a tax free loan of £10,000 and did not charge the employee any interest.[18]

Entertainment

Your company can pay up to £150 per person per annum for staff celebration events such as a Christmas party (the total of £150 can't be exceeded). If you spend more than a total of £150 (even where you have several events), the entire amount becomes taxable.

Employee retail discounts and benefits

You can also provide directors and employees with discounts to restaurants, high street shopping, gyms etc. via a company called Perkbox (Perkbox.com).

As a director, you can also receive £300 gift vouchers from your limited company, but they cannot be exchangeable into cash. The types of gift vouchers are for high street shops and restaurants. This tax-free benefit may also be used in conjunction with Perkbox where discounts to high street shops and restaurants are also provided.

---

18 A benefit in kind is an income tax charge and an employer's national insurance charge of 13.8% paid by the company. In the above example the £10,000 loan should have an interest charge of 3.25% being £325. If the company does not charge the employee this amount, the employee is taxed £325 x their income tax band and the company pays national insurance of 13.8% x £325 being £44.85.

CHAPTER 9

PROPERTY MANAGEMENT AND LANDLORD ESSENTIALS

One aspect of property investment that puts some people off is the idea of being a landlord and having to manage issues like maintenance, repairs and tenant disputes. This is a valid concern but there are ways to address this. The first is to put measures in place, so your experience of being a landlord is as stress free as possible. There are five key areas to consider.

1. **Get educated.** Learning as much as you can about being a landlord and your responsibilities is imperative. Even if you're a landlord already, I recommend the one-day landlord accreditation course run by the National Landlords Association (NLA).[19] It costs about £100 and is a great way of learning about the most important aspects of being a landlord and becoming an accredited landlord. If you join the NLA (also approximately £100 per year), you can become an accredited landlord for free by completing their online course modules at your own pace. The NLA also run a other useful courses on subjects such as tenant eviction and portable appliance testing for landlords.

2. **Outsource tasks you don't want to do.** Make a list of all the tasks you can think of pertaining to preparing, letting and managing your property. Identifying those you can't or don't want to do means you can find ways to delegate and outsource them (if this is affordable) and avoid doing things you hate or are too time consuming. However, it's always useful to do a task at least once, as it might give you valuable experience (particularly when it comes to training other staff members).

---

19 Find out more here: National Landlords Association, https://landlords.org.uk/ [accessed 11th November 2018]

You can outsource anything these days such as: putting furniture together, painting and decorating, cleaning, creating tenant adverts, doing viewings, processing credit and reference checks and much more. Remember that the time you spend doing low value activities may come at the cost of missing out on high value opportunities.

3. **Focus on one strategy at a time (if possible).** One benefit of focusing on just one or two strategies is the expertise you can quickly build up in that area and the economy of scale that comes with managing a portfolio of the same type of property. By sticking to the same strategy, you can more easily and effectively source new properties of the same kind, find tenants, manage the property, fix maintenance issues and find staff who can easily work across different properties (for example). This is true for any strategy, but particularly for HMOs which generally require higher maintenance and resources but due to the strong cash flow are considered higher reward and worthwhile!

4. **Communication skills.** Ensuring that communication between yourself, the tenants and any others involved (for example, property manager) is optimum from the start and is invaluable. This includes clearly communicating house rules or important parts of the rental agreement to the tenant from the start, ensuring important conversations (for example, about damage to the property or giving notice to terminate the contract) are documented, and gaining a clear understanding of the responsibilities of the tenant or landlord (for example, gardening costs). Clear and regular communication can prevent problems arising throughout a tenancy or misunderstandings occurring.

5. **Systemising and outsourcing your property business.** Busy doctors are often time poor so it's important to put in place some systems (even if you only have one property) to ensure important things don't get forgotten and you fulfil your obligations as a landlord. This includes registering your tenant's deposit in a timely manner or returning it to them, paying utility bills, managing a broken boiler quickly, or making plans for viewings when a tenant's tenancy ends and they move out. There are many ways to deal with this using landlord software with built in reminders, apps, virtual assistants and property managers to ensure your experience of being a landlord or managing your properties is smooth and straightforward. Ensuring you set time aside each month to review your property or portfolio is a good way to stay on track.

Dr Steve Day is an absolute expert when it comes to systems and outsourcing. In fact, his expertise in the area was developed through pure necessity in managing his own portfolio.

CASE STUDY

Steve Day: 'retired' A&E doctor, from Manchester

Lives in Stockholm, Sweden

I finished a degree in computing in 2002 and started to build my property portfolio. Being time rich and cash poor, I did everything myself. Sourcing, buying, renovating, letting, maintaining, decorating, cleaning, bookkeeping, accounts ... I was a true one-man-band! I saved a few quid but totally limited the potential of my property business. At twenty lettable units I reached my capacity and decided that was all I could cope with. I was tired and needed a break, so I decided to train as a doctor instead!

Despite the additional workload, I was too stubborn to get help. I thought, 'Why should I pay 10% for a letting agent when all they do is a few viewings and a couple of contracts?' For the first five years, I winged it. The problem was, I have a terrible memory, so every year was like starting from scratch and I often forgot things or wasted time repeating tasks. I needed a system and started to keep records and checklists for everything I did, and found contractors to help me during the busiest times who followed these checklists. This halved the time it took me to do the admin.

By 2015 I'd been working as a doctor for four years, still juggling two careers I was burnt out. I ended up working as a part-time locum, trying to grow my property portfolio and considering whether or not to enter specialist training. I was exhausted, and each property I bought added to the problem.

I desperately needed help. In 2016 I hired my first property and business mentor. I read books and attended courses in property management, systemisation and outsourcing. I had loved systems analysis and design during my computing degree, but I'd never thought to apply it to my

Thinking about what is involved in your own property investmen own business. That year I started mapping out my business processes so other people could follow them.

The real light-bulb moment was when I took on my first virtual assistant, and got them to do my admin and property sourcing work for me on an ad-hoc basis. There was no contract, no PAYE and no commitment, and they charged only £6 per hour. By simply watching the videos I'd created and following my checklists she was able to take over much of my day-to-day work. I now run my portfolio in less than an hour a week and never have to answer calls or emails about my properties and we run almost 100% occupancy thanks to the systems I have built.

I'm a geek at heart and I quickly became hooked on creating workflows and operations manuals and outsourcing my work. I shared my ideas and progress on Facebook and soon had people asking for help. The next thing I knew I'd set-up an online training course to help other property investors systemise and outsource their work. One of my first clients, Kevin, went from sixty-plus hours a week to six hours a month running ninety-six properties, proving that a simple approach to systemising and outsourcing can work for both small players like me and bigger outfits such as Kevin's.

I had toyed with the idea of quitting medicine for a couple of years but felt ashamed and pressured by friends and family to stick at it. I also doubted I'd find such a rewarding career, one that would give me that amazing feeling you get when you help a patient in need. However, I feel I have it in the most unlikely of places. Following my passion for systems means I now help others to free their time to spend doing whatever they will help you identify any group tasks and create systems for those tasks. For example, the following are the different parts involved in letting a property:

- **Preparation for letting**: cleaning; furnishing; photography; agent valuations or price research; advertising.
- **Filling property**: finding tenants (or a lettings agent); carrying out viewings; reference checking tenants; signing rental agreements; collecting and transfering deposits and rent; doing tenant check-ins or check-outs
- **Cleaning and maintenance**: cleaning, maintenance checks (for example, gutters or regular inspections—3-6 monthly); problems and repairs troubleshooting; monitoring annual service dates for gas or electrical appliances.
- **Finances**: rent collection; payment of utilities and service charges; payment of other expenses (for example, insurance); maintenance; repairs; management; monitoring upcoming tenancy expiration dates and communicating with tenants.

You might be someone who *really* doesn't want to deal with tenants. If so, fear not as there are strategies you can use.

1. You could pay for your properties to be let and fully managed by agents which puts tenants and management issues at arm's length. Bear in mind you will still be contacted by agents about issues and any decisions regarding repairs.

2. You may enter into a joint venture project where your partner deals with all matters to do with tenants and maintenance while you take responsibility for some other aspect *for example, refurb or funding).

3. You could go into property development and build houses to be sold rather than rented.

4. You could source great property projects and sell them on to developers or investors for a fee.

5. Or, like one tech savvy doctor has done (in the case study below), you could set up an entire business to outsource every single task so that you only have to oversee the systems and staff managing the tasks!

CASE STUDY

Dr Sayinthen Vivekanantham: ST1 academic radiology, Nottingham

I first got into property back during the last recession when the markets collapsed. This was probably the best time to get into the market due to the huge fall in house prices. After the economic downturn, my family and I bought a three bedroom flat in Redhill for £135,000 which we converted into four bedrooms and used as an HMO. This happened by accident as we originally tried to let the whole property as a single-let until one tenant came for a viewing and asked if he could rent just one room. A lot of people had lost their jobs at that time and couldn't afford to rent a whole place, so room lets were an economical way of living. We realised that by renting out four rooms separately we would receive more income than renting out the whole flat, and that was the start of my journey into HMOs! The market rent for a three-bed flat at that time was £900 per month without bills and we were offered £500-600 per month including bills for a double room, so by renting out four rooms we would more than double the rental income of a single let property.

Rental income provided us with good cash flow and the capital needed to keep investing in property. In addition, as the capital value of the property increased over time, we decided to release equity through a re-mortgage and purchase other property that we ran as HMOs.

Since then we have diversified further into serviced apartments (SA). We run SA for our properties and for those of others too, with automated systems built so we can invest in property anywhere in the UK and have them managed by our internal staff and teams. Through using the systems we have set up for ourselves, we have the capacity to source and manage investment properties for investors, too!

Property has given me financial freedom that means I don't need to rely on the day job. I now go into my day job as a radiology trainee out of a passion for the job rather than for being concerned about working to survive. Financial pressure can reduce the enjoyability of the job, and a secondary income can help you achieve more enjoyment from your main line of work, whether that is medicine or another career! I am now passionate about helping other people achieve this through our investment services.

However, it's not a hands-off investment if you are doing it yourself. It's an investment with a period of learning and potential to make mistakes if you don't have someone to guide you, but it's a wise investment you can build up and create strong cash flow from with the know-how. Any business can be time intense, and I see property as somewhere between a business and an investment. The great thing is that if you work with the right systems and teams, it can become passive.

As a person I'm incredibly risk averse, but I appreciate you have to invest your money to build up a passive income. In my view it is the best asset class for growing wealth sustainably with minimal risk. I say this, as I feel other asset classes come with much more risk (for example, shares go up and down on a daily basis; with property this is more gradual and predictable). Property can also provide multiple sources of income (for example, rental income and capital appreciation).

I've learned a lot of business skills from doing property and translational skills that I apply to management positions in my career and other business ventures I am involved with. Property gives you the opportunity to harness and practice these skills, and I recommend it to all doctors thinking of investing in property as a long-term asset.

CHAPTER 10

THE PAINS AND PITFALLS OF PROPERTY INVESTING AND HOW TO AVOID THEM!

In this chapter we consider some common pains and pitfalls associated with property investment. While some of the potential pitfalls (for example, buying off-plan, at auction and abroad) come with a caution warning, you shouldn't be put off altogether but apply good common-sense principles.

Not doing enough due diligence

One of the most common mistakes people make when investing in property is not doing enough due diligence. Even when a professional property sourcer sends me a deal, I still do my own due diligence on the property to investigate whether the deal meets my personal requirements and to verify that the information about the deal being sold to me is accurate. This is a vital part of the process and corners should never be cut. Spending a little more time and money during this part of the process can save you thousands compared to making a bad investment decision, which could cost you a lot of money after it's too late.

TOP TIP

Create a due diligence form or spreadsheet to help you do due diligence and adequately assess every deal that comes under your nose.

Not having finance ready

Many investors overlook the importance of having funds in place for a property purchase or underestimate the time it can take to obtain mortgage finance. Although I know several investors who find deals and then go looking for the cash to fund them, I don't recommend this approach unless you have a network of contacts that can help your secure finance under pressure. This is particularly important in markets where you face fierce competition from cash buyers and developers who may be able to move faster than you, offering a faster sale to the vendor. It pays off to be organised and appear ready and committed to buy.

The process for obtaining mortgage finance has become much more complicated in the current economic climate and far more detailed information and checks are required from borrowers by the lenders. As a result, mortgage applications can take significantly longer (in some cases up to six weeks before obtaining a formal offer). This exposes you to being dropped by the vendor or gazumped by someone who can move faster or make a higher offer.

Speed and certainty can be vital in competitive markets or in situations of urgency (for example, when dealing with vendors who need to sell fast). If you're not able to provide this speed and certainty, you may lose a good deal. It pays to be organised when it comes to financing your transaction.

TOP TIP

If using mortgage finance, try to have the following documents available when you start viewing properties: -

- Proof of deposit funds (POF) letter from your bank/solicitor/accountant
- Decision in principle (DIP) formal mortgage offer from your lender for the type of property you want to buy
- Letter from your mortgage broker supporting your position to purchase

If using private finance (for example, funds from a joint venture partner) you will just need a POF letter.

Overpaying on a property due to buyer's psychology

Buying a property can be an emotional process, and until you learn to view property investment as a business transaction, it'is easy to react to competition by increasing your bid until you 'win'. This is common in auction rooms where the seemingly cool as a cucumber bidder becomes increasingly competitive and emotional over losing the prospective ownership of 'their' property (which they have become increasingly attached to throughout the bidding process). How can we protect ourselves against this?

A crucial part of the due diligence process is evaluating what the property is worth and whether it fits with your strategy. If so, you must decide prior to making your first offer what the absolute maximum price you can afford to pay is (having budgeted for stamp duty, legal fees and any refurbishment work). Once you've calculated your maximum price, never make an offer over this amount. Having clear rules and criteria to stick to will make your purchase decisions and property business easier and more successful over the long term. The great thing about property is that there is always another deal around the corner, so be strict with your criteria and be patient. It's a numbers game and you will eventually find the deal you are looking for. Persistence is key here.

TOP TIP

Decide on your maximum price you are willing to pay before you start the offer or bidding process and NEVER go over this

Buying without viewing

There may be exceptions to this rule when you become an experienced investor or know your market and area inside out, however, until you reach this level, never, EVER buy a property without viewing it. This may seem obvious, but I've heard of plenty of people buying properties without having viewed them and getting a nasty shock once they discover they've bought a lemon. Clever photography and elaborate descriptions can help to disguise problem properties. For example, a property may be across the road from a noisy railway line, suffer from structural problems, be inhabited by squatters or a regulated tenant (who have the legal right to remain in the property paying an extremely low rent) or any number of nightmarish situations you may not be aware of unless you physically view a place. You can discover a great deal about a property by speaking to the owners, eighbours and locals, and the information gathered can be invaluable, not to mention the rapport you should develop with the agent who may become one of your key contacts in future.

TOP TIP

- Decide on your maximum price you are willing to pay before you start the offer or bidding process and NEVER go over this

Buying off plan/abroad/new build

Although many investors successfully buy off-plan/new builds or buy properties abroad, to date I have never done so and following several discussions with experienced investors about the matter, I would err on the side of caution for the reasons below. Please note that if you are interested in *building* or *developing* new build properties, this is something completely different. What we are discussing here is *buying* an apartment off plan or buying a property in a new building (a property less than ten years old, for example).

Buying new builds

Although I do know people who have bought new build properties and have experienced an increase in the value of their properties, this does seem to be area dependent. For example, many investors who bought in East London around the time of Olympics have benefited from the significant development and improvements to East London since then. Property is in high demand in London and average prices have risen. However, I recently reviewed a property my friend was considering buying in Greenwich in London. The flat was in a beautiful new building, brand new and with fantastic views. However, looking at the price history of the flats in the building we could see that the prices hadn't moved in over five years. The reason for this could be a lack of demand driving prices down or the prices being over-inflated at the launch of the new build development and being sold over market value (OMV) hence no evidence of market increase, or a decrease in house prices over a five-year period followed by increase causing prices to appear the same.

With new builds it's often hard to find comparables which help you to understand the real and projected market value of new build properties since they are new to the market, with no historical sales data. This is risky because comparable data may not exist. It's more challenging to assess what you're buying and you may need to make assumptions.

It's also worth bearing in mind that developers build and sell properties for a profit, therefore these properties are rarely cheap or below market value (BMV). A common strategy is for developers to inflate prices and offer them to buyers at a 'discount', which in reality may not be a discount at all.

Another consideration is that in most cases, there are fewer or in some cases zero opportunities to add value to new builds and in so doing increase the value of the property. Why should this matter? Well, if you are buying a property to let and hold or use long-term it may not matter at all; it depends on your personal investment strategy. However, if you like to keep your options open, you may want to be able to sell for profit or refinance some equity out of the property in the future. Some people who buy new builds are not able to do this as they may have bought an overpriced property to start with, the market growth may have been slower than predicted, or the property market may be experiencing a dip. Depending on their circumstances, they may be unable to sell for a profit for a long time (with cash locked up in the property) or be forced to sell at a loss.

Buying off-plan property

Off-plan builds have not yet been built or may not yet be completed. This means the cash you provide for a deposit or purchase will be tied up and inaccessible for a potentially long time, meaning you will miss out on leveraging it elsewhere. You must also accept that while waiting for your property to be built, the property market may change and you may be exposed in some way (for example, decline in tenants looking to rent or decline in buyers). Recent property tax changes, Brexit and immigration policies are a good example of how external factors can affect the property market. Always make sure you have several back-up plans to protect your investment. On the flip side, buying off-plan properties in the right market can be an extraordinarily good way to leverage your cash and generate great profits. For example, it's possible to pay a small deposit for a property and sell the property on to another buyer without ever completing on the purchase or paying any stamp duty yourself. This is done using what is called an *assignable contract* and allows you to benefit from any capital appreciation during a rising market.

You must also consider the track record of the developers and what other projects they have completed, if they were completed on time, and whether they kept to budget or ran into debts. The last thing you want is to invest money in a development and find that the contractor has gone bust!

CASE STUDY

Dr Zoe Malik Kemp, GP trainee and property investor, London

Zoe started her property endeavours with her first purchase, over ten years ago. Realising that she and her husband Roo would have a lot to pay in rental payments for several years if waiting until she was a doctor to own their own property, she started researching further.

After the 2008 financial crash, Zoe came across the concept of owning 3+1 properties to enable financial freedom. This idea is based on having one residential and three buy to let properties to facilitate your journey. In employing and developing the ideas of this strategy, Zoe and Roo decided that off-plan purchases could work within this model.

One example of an off-plan purchase they made was in a major town centre, thirty minutes to central London. They were eager to invest at that point but had little personal time to do so. They also did not have all of the required capital upfront, but knew that within a couple of years, they could save it. They therefore found a company able to assist them in the purchase, who carried out the due diligence on the property and the area, including plans for regeneration, current sales prices and current rental prices, and negotiated the deal for them in return for a finder's fee. Zoe and Roo reserved the property with a small deposit and liked the ability to be able to pay the remainder of the purchase deposit in stages prior to the property completing. As contracts were exchanged early on, and completion was delayed until the property was built, they locked in the price of the property over two years prior to the completion. This enabled accumulation of value during that two years, which worked well to their advantage. They were then able to release all their money put into the property within six months during which time the property was let, generating an income and continuing to be held for ongoing income generation from rent and future capital growth gains over the mid-long term.

Key figures from this example are listed below:

Purchase price: £164,000

Reservation fee: £2,000

Finder's fee (approx. 2.5% + VAT): £5,000

Subsequent (delayed) deposits (in this example 10% less reservation fee + 5%): £14,400 + £8,200

Further deposit on completion (15%): £24,600

Mortgage on completion (70% LTV): £114,800

Therefore, money put into the deal: £54,200

Valuation after six months: £285,000

Re-mortgage amount (70% LTV): £199,500

Money released: £84,700

Return on capital invested (ROCI): ((84,700-54200)/84,700) x 100=36%

N.B. Associated purchase costs such as SDLT (Stamp Duty Land Tax) and legal fees have also been omitted. SDLT has also been reformed subsequent to the exchange of contracts of the above purchase and each case should be considered individually.

(Warning; this can be a high risk/high reward strategy with figures working to your disadvantage if property values decrease in the period you are awaiting completion and prior to re-mortgaging).

Zoe's property investments have enabled her and Roo to be confident in their retirement planning and in leaving a legacy for future generations. She has improved her existing transferable skills and developed others including prioritisation of tasks and overcoming perfectionism, whilst maintaining high standards. Zoe is optimistic about the future. She looks forward to completing her GP training and having a portfolio career to enable her medical and property passions.

Zoe and Roo have their own business, which acquires property, project manages major refurbishments and developments and manages portfolios for other investors. They also own a Serviced Accommodation business which is expanding its client base providing full management for serviced accommodation to property owners. Their current buy, refurbish, remortgage (BRR) project has a GDV (gross development value (GDV) of £1,500,000 and is due to finish later this year. Zoe and Roo are now also looking at bringing their own off-plan opportunities to the professional market.

Buying abroad

Buying abroad can be as good an investment as buying at home, but only if you know the market and local area and you have a clear investment plan. Perhaps you want to invest abroad to have a holiday home you can rent or own for personal use. Whatever the reason, be aware that you may have to factor in:

- Currency exchange rates and how changes in the strength of the currency against your local currency may affect your investment
- Foreign currency mortgages (if applicable)
- Service charges, letting fees, management fees, cleaning fees
- Additional travel expenses if you need to travel to visit the property
- The general hassle factor if you don't have someone you can trust to look after the property while you're not there

With foreign properties, the fact of the matter is that you may not have adequate local knowledge of the property market to fully assess the investment. It can be tedious, and expensive and stressful to manage a property in another town/city let alone another country considering factors such as language barriers, differences in property laws etc. Naturally, there are ways around this, but it's worth thinking twice before jumping on this bandwagon!

TOP TIPS

If you're buying a new build/off-plan/foreign property you can minimise your risk by ensuring you:

1. Know which part of the property market cycle you are in (rising or falling?)

2.Have local knowledge of the area (or access to it from a trustworthy source)

3. Know what the property will be worth after it is built (what are market predictions for house prices for the next few years)

4. Know what strategy you are using (are you buying to flip, use as a HMO or other?)

5. Know your exit strategies (would you be able to sell at a profit, to another investor or hold long-term if required?)

6. Get several opinions/valuations from different agents

7. Ideally, always buy at a true discount to have a buffer against any losses; have decent comparables or multiple opinions from different agents before going ahead

It may well be that you buy off-plan at the right time and benefit from the increase in value of the build due to being in a rising market. For example, you may expect property values to be increasing by 5% per annum. Several friends of mine have been lucky enough to buy in good areas and benefit from an immediate uplift in value. However, I also know people who have lost out and have to sell either at a loss or just break even.

Buying a bargain at auction

Buying at auction can be a great way to find excellent investment properties but be warned, auction properties appear cheap for many reasons. Properties at auction usually have some sort of problem such as dilapidation, a short lease or sitting tenants, or building work may have been undertaken without planning permission. If you want to buy a property at auction, do so with caution and make sure you visit the property, read the legal pack provided, and obtain legal advice before purchase. Take care not to get sucked into a bidding war in the auction room, as the auctioneer will encourage you to keep bidding to achieve the highest price for the vendor.

TOP TIP

Legal packs for auction properties are often not released until a week or two before the date of the auction. If buying at auction, ensure you have an experience solicitor ready to quickly (and economically) assess the legal pack of any potential properties and make you aware of any risks. This will give you the confidence and certainty you require to place bids in the auction room.

Not planning your exit

Property is a secure investment. However, you should always plan for the worst and have an action plan you can follow if things go wrong. For each property investment or project, you should have three exit strategies. This is even more important if you are working with a JV partner who finances the project and who may want their cash back in the future. For example, if you're buying a property using joint venture finance and your partner later wants to get their funds back out, your three exit scenarios may be as follows:

1. Refinance investor cash out (this may be possible if you are adding value to the property and can re-mortgage based on the increased value of the property)
2. Replace the investor's funds with that of another investor
3. Sell the property

TOP TIP

Look after the downside and the upside will take care of itself. Always plan for the worst-case scenario and ask yourself what you will do if your Number 1 plan for the property investment fails.

Giving up too early

This is extremely common. Most people give up before they have even started because they don't have the sufficient knowledge, network, support or access to funds. They remain in what design thinkers call the *ideation phase*, forever *thinking* about doing something without ever taking action and implementing it. Some people will go years before they make their first brave step into the world of property. Also, while successfully investing does not take long (from thirty days to twelve months is realistic, depending on your strategy), it is not get rich quick and while you may be excited and impatient to get started, you need to give it some time before you can reap the fruits of your labour.

TOP TIP

Get connected to your main reasons or motivations for investing. If it's important enough to you, be decisive and make it an absolute priority to take action regularly and consistently (it may be in baby steps such as listening to one webinar or audiobook a week or you may give it your all, viewing up to forty properties a week), get educated, surround yourself with like-minded people who inspire you and share the same interest or vision, get help and support from people who are more experienced than you and start to broaden your network.

CHAPTER 11

OPPORTUNITIES RIGHT UNDER YOUR DOCTOR'S NOSE

There may be opportunities sitting right under your nose, real estate strategies within the healthcare field. As doctors we often have unique insights into the problems in our healthcare system, but we also have insights into the problems in housing and social care affecting our patients. We are therefore in a perfect position to brainstorm solutions for these problems and engage in projects which have a significant social impact. For this reason, it's worth keeping your eyes open to the property problems going on around you, and with the knowledge you're building up about property investment, thinking about whether there might be some viable solutions.

You might also decide to do some private practice during your careers or even run your own practice. If you're a GP, you might consider purchasing your own practice premises, and a knowledge of commercial property investment will be imperative, as it would be for anyone interested in setting up community healthcare or wellness services. Below are some ideas (by the way, don't forget me in your will when you become rich and famous!).

You might also decide to do some private practice during your careers or even run your own practice. If you're a GP, you might consider purchasing your own practice premises, and a knowledge of commercial property investment will be imperative, as it would be for anyone interested in setting up community healthcare or wellness services. Below are some ideas (by the way, don't forget me in your will when you become rich and famous!).

Using rent to rent to set up a health or wellness clinic

A few years ago, I stayed in an Airbnb belonging to a psychologist living in London. We got talking about property as she enjoyed a good side income through letting her two-bed flat on Airbnb, and she told me that she also rented a property in central London where she ran her clinic and sublet the rooms to other psychologists for their clinics. I was amazed this lady was basically doing rent to rent within the commercial field—I'd never considered this! She fell into this accidentally as she couldn't afford to buy a property to set up her business and looked into whether she could rent one instead. Slowly but surely, it became a successful business. In fact, a lot of people 'accidentally' fall upon strategies through their efforts brainstorming creative solutions to problems.

Health tourism

The health 'tourism' industry is an interesting niche market. You might be providing a solution for patients recuperating after a hospital stay or procedure, relatives of patients, or even patients with special needs.

One example is an innovative start-up based out of London called Accomable which focused on travel listings that were disabled-friendly. The founders of Accomable (who both have spinal muscular atrophy and use wheelchairs) were frustrated at the difficulty they encountered in planning accommodation, travel and activities around their accessibility needs and decided they could create an easy tech solution for this. What a fantastic idea! They were inundated with customers, demand far exceeded supply, and they were unsurprisingly soon snapped up by Airbnb!

In terms of accommodation for the relatives of patients undergoing hospital treatment, there are multiple opportunities in areas where there is a lot of health tourism or demand for other reasons. Typically, you will want to focus on properties or sites close to the hospital and suitable for short stays, but you may consider alternatives such as respite holiday homes. I regularly see adverts on hospital notice boards for accommodation available for patient relatives at one of the London hospitals I work at. Some hospitals work in partnership with charities and other accommodation providers to support relatives and patients who may be travelling from another town, city or even from abroad for medical care.

Solutions to the NHS bed blocking crisis

One novel solution to the bed blocking in the NHS is a company set up by my mentor Paul Gaudin on the NHS Clinical Entrepreneur Programme. Along with fellow clinical entrepreneur Harry Thirkettle, Paul set up a business called *Care Rooms* in an attempt to provide a solution to the bed-blocking crisis in the NHS. Care Rooms provides low support care to people who are well enough to leave hospital but perhaps not well enough to be at home alone (see www.carerooms.com). It's like an Airbnb for people with a spare room who can provide low support to patients such as warm meals and perhaps basic care, and receive an income for the rent of the room and care provided.

Accommodation providing care

Life expectancy is higher than ever before and we have an increasing ageing population that at some point might require extra support or care at home. While nursing homes is a well-established sector (unfortunately with variable levels of 'care') there is another rapidly rising sector that could be of interest. This is the *assisted living* sector which supports people (of varying ages and abilities), providing them with different levels of care. Some companies working in the assisted living sector have created whole retirement villages with different types of accommodation on offer, ranging from properties suitable for independent people to nursing accommodation with state-of-the-art facilities, health monitoring technology and top-quality healthcare staff.

Our experience as healthcare professionals within this sector could be invaluable in planning and designing high quality and appropriate care for the end user. Working in a healthcare service where provided treatment is based on evidence and clinical need sets us apart from organisations that are profit driven (and whose staff are also required to be). There's nothing wrong with making money; it's a tool like anything else in life and a business must be financially viable to deserve your efforts. However, if you focus on your passion for providing and creating an amazing product or service rather than making a ton of money, financial success will come naturally.

Setting up a GP surgery

Within the population of doctors working in the NHS, setting up a GP surgery is probably the most common experience doctors might have after purchasing their own home or buy to let. It's certainly not a straightforward business and I'm not going to get into the different types of contracts required to run an NHS GP surgery here as this is outside the scope of this book, but generally speaking, you need to have a GMS, PMS or APMS contract to set up and open an NHS GP practice. Once a contract is in place, GP partners have the option to rent a premises from a private landlord to run their practice from or purchase it. There are also a number of GP premises or healthcentres built and owned by a third party such as NHS properties.

Assuming the GP partners have a contract to provide primary care services, they would look for a premises to rent or purchase, and run their practice from it. The premises could be a residential property, or it could be a commercial premises such as a retail unit. Both types of property might require refurbishment to create the standard or layout required for clinical work.

Renting a GP premises

If you rent practice premises owned by the NHS, you have to pay both the rent and the service charges for the premises. When the GP surgery rents premises, the clinical commissioning group

(CCG) appoint a valuer to report on what is a fair rent to pay and this valuation will be passed on to the landlord. The GP surgery can apply for *leasehold cost reimbursements* to cover the cost of the rent, but can never take any profit from rent received from CCG which is paid to the landlord. If the premises requires refurbishment, the CCG will usually only contribute towards the cost of this in exceptional circumstances, but sometimes CCG *improvement grants* can be applied for. Depending on the contract between tenant (GP partners) and landlord (NHS), maintenance issues might be paid for and resolved by NHS contractors or by the practice.

Purchasing a GP premises

Alternatively, the partners could purchase a GP premises privately using their own funds and rent this to their own GP surgery for a fair market rent. Again, a valuer would be instructed to determine a fair rent called *notional rent* and the GP practice to apply for notional rent reimbursements. In this situation, it's possible for the GP partners to make a profit from the rental income reimbursement received from the CCG (for example, if the mortgage cost is lower than the notional rent they would generate a profit). Therefore, it makes more financial sense to own your GP practice premises than to rent it.

If the property requires refurbishment, it's possible to apply for grants to part-fund the refurbishment. For example, NHS England has a fund that will provide 75% of the cost of refurbishments such as extensions and facilities that will allow the practice to expand or provide more services to the community. One of my clients recently put a business case together and was successful in getting funding for her practice in West London. She kindly took me on a tour of the practice run by her and her father and I saw first hand the amazing new services (minor surgery, dermatology and paediatric clinic facilities) they will now be offering their community from the practice. The increase in space adds value in two ways. Firstly, the value of the building will now be worth more due to it being larger (bricks and mortar value), and secondly, the market rent (or notional rent) value will also be higher.

For many people with access to deposit funds, investing in your own GP premises is a no brainer as you can benefit from capital appreciation and rental income over a long period of time and have complete control (subject to contractual agreements) over what you do with the property long-term.

However, running a GP practice (or any healthcare service for that matter) is a challenging and complicated business due to the healthcare ecosystem we currently live and work in. More practices are having to deliver more care for sicker patients with smaller budgets, and for many small practices this can become unsustainable. Because of this issue, several companies throughout the UK have emerged who are able to take over the running of a GP practice or help to merge several small practices to manage them more efficiently and cost effectively due to economies of scale.

It's not all doom and gloom, though. Dr Rahul Sahay and his sister Dr Priya Rischie are GPs from Birmingham who together with their family, not only saved, but expanded their GP practice, using some pretty advanced property strategies quite by accident! Rahul kindly shared their story with me which I found so inspiring that I wanted to share it with you here.

CASE STUDY

Dr Rahul Sahay: GP and property investor from Birmingham

In 2013 I got involved in a property project that transformed the way I think about property and investment forever. Before then, my only prior property experience was buying a house off-plan in 2006/07 (just before the crash!) with the aim of living there when I got married. However, once it was built, I ended up renting it out for two years before moving there in March 2011. We stayed there for five years and ideally wanted to sell it, but as an investment property the numbers didn't stack up for that house so we are still renting it out.

Meanwhile, my journey into property investment occurred as a result of me being a GP in our family-run practice. Our small GP surgery was located in a derelict council school building, and in mid-2013, the council told us they were knocking down the site to rebuild the school. We had six months to vacate the premises and a very stressful period followed of trying to find new premises.

We noticed a large property close to our existing surgery with four commercial units on the ground floor and six flats above. One of the retail units was empty which we hoped to run our surgery out of. The other three were occupied (one by the post office who were leaving, the second by a tenant who was months behind on his rent and also dealing drugs, the third and biggest unit was empty and had been a former snooker hall closed down by the police due to drugs). By chance, my mum (who is also our practice manager) discovered who the landlord was we arranged to meet him.

We wanted to rent out one of the retail units to refurb into our small GP surgery, but we ended up talking about buying the whole site. The vendor's asking price was £750,000. We were fumbling in the darkness about the value, so arranged an independent valuation. The surveyor valued the property at £550,000, significantly lower than the asking price but still a price we could not afford. Furthermore, the six flats had been left in a terrible state by the tenants and most of those in the ground floor retail units were dealing drugs, so we would need to evict them and do a complete refurbishment, which would increase the cost!

After much discussion, we agreed we didn't want to be tenants at the mercy of a landlord again, running the risk relocation in the future. The costs of refurbishing a premises to become a GP surgery are significant and also has to be covered by you so we wanted to mitigate this risk by buying. We went back to the landlord and agreed to meet in the middle at £650,000 purchase price.

We approached our bank for a mortgage but they weren't interested due to the poor condition of the property. So, we changed course and over the next twelve months, entered into what we now know was a lease option agreement with the vendor. This happened after we suggested paying him £3,000 per month whilst we did up the building and had permission to rent it out. Any surplus rent generated, we would keep.

Neither of us knew the official term lease option agreement for this – our solicitors sorted it out. We wanted to carry out the work and see whether we could persuade the bank to give us a mortgage to buy the building.

With six flats let and our GP surgery running, we got another bank valuation. The former post office and snooker hall were empty and the valuation came in at £350,000 - even less than the valuation the surveyor made!

Disappointed, but seeing the value the place had and already having made a financial investment we negotiated again with the vendor who agreed to allow us to purchase and slowly pay down the £650,000 over a period of seven years. Together myself, my parents and sister pulled together a £300,000 deposit (a combination of equity release and savings) and entered into a financial agreement to pay the remaining money back over seven years at 3.5% over the base rate per annum. This sort of arrangement is called vendor finance, as the vendor in theory is loaning you the funds you need to purchase a property. Once again, we didn't know that was a strategy and thought we were doing something unusual by asking him! We wanted to make the deal work and the vendor was also doing everything he could to help us!

By this point the residential units were up and running and our GP surgery was expanding rapidly. We decided to use the remaining time to extend our surgery into the next retail unit and also refurbished the former snooker hall and leased it out to a reputable charity shop.

Two years into the vendor finance agreement, we approached our bank again as we wanted to own the building, so we could use it as a vehicle to get us on the property ladder and invest further. At this point, all six flats were in a decent state and fully let while downstairs a charity shop was renting one of the retail units and our surgery occupied the other three. This time, our bank valued it at £1.2m! We hadn't expected a result like this, and needless to say, we were overjoyed. Finally, we could take out a proper mortgage over a longer period of time and pay the landlord everything he was owed.

One of the learning points this experience highlighted to me is the importance of building a rapport with the vendor. A key factor in our success was that both sides wanted to make the deal work and we were fortunate to have met an amazing and kind person. So much so, that my father and I went to Wales yesterday and spent the day with him and his wife!

Reflecting on this experience, I can say that property has opened a lot of avenues for me. I have developed my business skills further and we have been able to grow a vital community service as well as a long-term cash-flowing asset we have complete control over.

In March 2018 our lender released the equity from the building to us (£200,000 unsecured) which we have used to buy a cashflowing HMO. It hasn't been an easy journey by any means and it has been a steep but exciting learning curve but now I've got the bug, I'm keeping my eyes open for my next project!

Commercial conversion of healthcare property to residential

There are several benefits to buying commercial properties, including taxation, expenses, investing through pension funds and creating multiple streams of property income through residential and commercial rents.

You might come across GP surgeries or nursing homes for sale that most people would not be interested in (unless they're developers or have adequate knowledge to take advantage of the opportunity). If such buildings aren't purchased for a healthcare service use, they can often be converted into houses or flats. In fact, it's common to come across beautiful buildings that were former hospitals, police stations or even prisons!

If commercial property is an area you would be interested in, keep your eyes wide open while you're at your day job, as you might come across a real gem. Don't forget that if you're going to need planning permission for a project, you can use a purchase option or purchase lease option to control the site while you apply for planning. For such building or development projects you need to know what you're doing, so always develop your knowledge first. Ideally, work with someone who has experience in the field and consult builders, architects, planning consultants and quantity surveyors who will help you bring the project together.

TOP TIPS

There are property investment opportunities everywhere. Once you've learned the basics, you can apply the same investment principles and strategies to solve problems within healthcare.

Beware of any conflict of interest that could arise due to your role as a doctor.

If investing in a GP surgery or buying into a practice, always consult with an accountant and valuer who specialises in this area of real estate.

As Winston Churchill said 'Never, ever, ever, ever, ever give up.' If you persevere for a project or cause that you believe in you can get amazing results.

FINAL WORDS

We are no strangers to education in the medical profession. However, the system often falls short when it comes to investing in our personal development and wellbeing, whether physical, mental or financial health. It's all very well being an amazing doctor but if it is at the cost of your health, relationships or financial stability there will come a point where it becomes detrimental. It's worth thinking about what kind of a life you want to lead, how you ideal work-life balance would look and being selective about what you invest your time in.

I hope this book has served to inspire and give you the confidence you need to move forward in property, whether to create the economic stability you need and deserve, make your money work harder or allow you to venture into an exciting project!

Investing in developing my property investment knowledge has been one of the best investments I have ever made and it has been life-changing in many ways. My advice to you following reading this book would be to use it as a catalyst to further your property investment knowledge. You can do this in many ways:

Networking events: There are many property networking events all over the country (and globally) and they are often a great place to start to meet people in the industry. These events are filled with a mixture of people from complete beginners to experienced investors as well as a variety of property professionals such as architects, developers, builders and more. Be aware that some events will be purely business networking with interesting talks while others will be set up to sell an investment or other product to the audience. Be careful if you ever attend an event of the latter kind and make sure you never hand over any money without taking independent financial advice. Unfortunately, there are still rogues in the industry who will take advantage of beginners.

Online networking: You may already be a member of our *Property Investing for Doctors* Facebook group. Online networks and groups can be handy when you need recommendations, have general property queries or want to meet other property investors in your area. Again, don't take financial advice from anyone online and never disclose your personal financial information in public—saying, for example, 'I have £10,000 in savings, what shall I do with it?' It may sound obvious to you but plenty of people do it and are subsequently preyed on!

Books, webinars and podcasts: There is a whole wealth of material available online. Some of it is free, but be aware that this does not mean it is up-to-date or reliable! However, you can learn a huge amount through reading or listening to property investment books and listening to popular property podcasts and webinars. If you face a long commute to work every day, this can be a great way to discover more about property and kill some time (Audible.com has quite a good selection of audio books on property and business).

Property conferences and shows: There are some fantastic annual conference events within the property investment and construction industry. I sometimes attend these to get ideas about building materials and design or to network with other professionals and listen to keynote speaker talks from leaders in the industry.

Property workshops and courses: At some point you might want to attend a property workshop or course. We run two popular property courses Eurekadoc (specifically for doctors) but there are a multitude of course available. Some courses will focus on a range of strategies while others will specialise on just one strategy or perhaps a particular skill related to property investment such as *creative funding* or *systemising your property business*. Make sure you do some research about the experience of trainers and ensure they are appropriately qualified.

Property coaching or mentoring: One reason people often fail at property investment is that after learning the theory of investing in property they fall short by not taking action. Sometimes this is due to uncertainty, fear, overwhelm or a lack of focus. Getting a good coach or mentor to support you can be a great way to kick-start your property journey and ensure you're held accountable to the actions required to achieve your goals. You should check your coach or mentor has a proven track record and get references from other people if possible. There are sometimes coaching or round-table groups you can join, to learn not only through your own experience but through observing the progress and experience of others. I have found this particularly useful within property and liken it to learning through cases in medicine where learning is consolidated through personal experience of managing a patient with a particular illness.

WHAT'S ON OFFER AT EUREKADOC?

One of my greatest passions in life is education. I am continually furthering my knowledge about property and I love to share the ingredients to success. The reason we have designed a range of resources at Eurekadoc is to help you to save you the time and uncertainty of searching for the knowledge, support and accountability you need succeed. With our support, you can achieve your goals, faster and easier than if you were doing it alone and you will enjoy the journey a lot more too.

Facebook group

We currently have over 700 members in our closed Facebook group. Join at https://www.facebook.com/groups/100334890630082/ to browse of the content, contribute to discussions and meet other doctor investors.

Webinars

We run regular webinars on property investment at Eurekadoc. To get pre-release information about these, make sure you sign-up to our mailing list at: www.eurekadoc.com

Face to face courses

We run a variety of face to face courses on property investing for doctors which you can browse here: https://www.eurekadoc.com/courses. The most popular are our Foundation Course (suitable for absolute beginners to more experienced investors) and our Advanced Course (suitable only for those who have a good knowledge of property investment and are looking to get into larger property projects or developments).

Online courses

If you can't make our face-to-face courses, why not take a look at our online options? We have our online property course available here: https://www.eurekadoc.com/online-courses and from time to time we run a fantastic live virtual course, during which you can interact with the speakers and delegates online and get any essential questions answered!

Property Accelerator Coaching Programme

This is a six-month coaching and accountability programme, suitable for doctors who are ready to accelerate their success. Applicants must demonstrate an appropriate level of prior knowledge or already be investing in property. The programme includes:

- Personal coaching session—orientation call to define your motivations, goals and steps required to achieve them
- Talent profiling test, report and de-brief session—identifying your personal strengths and weaknesses and how to select the best partners and strategies to enable your success
- Monthly Deep Dive tutorial—in depth property tutorial
- Monthly round table coaching—group coaching sessions to network and learn together
- Individual progress tracker—mapping your goals, successes and challenges.
- On demand recordings—unlimited access to Deep Dive and Coaching Call recordings for 12 months.
- Access to Lafina's personal team of property professionals
- 24/7 online support from Lafina and her team

For further information or to apply, please email: property@eurekadoc.com.

Your next steps

If you've enjoyed this book and are either new to investing or a little rusty, why not join one of our upcoming foundation courses? This will help you consolidate what you have learned in the book, and enable you to ask questions and smooth out any areas of uncertainty or confusion. You will also be able to meet like-minded doctors who are investing in property, discuss investment with our guest speakers and, ultimately, decide whether property is for you.

If you're more experienced and want guidance on how to get into more advanced property strategies such as property conversions and developments, our advanced course would be a great fit. After this, you should be absolutely clear about whether property investment is something you want to get started with and whether you might need a coach or a mentor.

Learn while investing

If you would like to get involved in one of our property crowdfunding projects which allows investors to experience the process first hand while we do the hard work and actively learn throughout the project. You can make sure you're informed of upcoming projects by emailing: property@eurekadoc.com.

BONUS CHAPTER

USEFUL RESOURCES

We have created this final bonus chapter packed full of useful resources for easy reference and to save you precious time! This chapter includes:

- Recommended property professionals and tradespeople
- Links to useful websites and resources
- Free bonus *Preparing to Invest* module
- Recommended exclusive discounts and offers for readers of *Property Investing for Doctors*

INVEST IN PROPERTY THE EASY WAY
Join the property lending revolution at
www.blendnetwork.com
Minimum investment only £1,000
Fixed returns UP TO 15% p.a.
Secured against property
Capital at risk
Register now in 2 minutes so that you can pick & choose from our available loans and start earning double-digit returns. It's very simple!
All loans are secured against first legal charge on the property.
No fees when you lend.
BLEND Loan Network Limited is an Appointed Representative of Resolution Compliance Ltd which is authorised and regulated by the Financial Conduct Authority (FRN. 574048).

Optimise.

OUR CLIENTS

Are you a property investor or a medical professional?

Are you frustrated or disgruntled with how much tax you're paying? Let us help build your wealth in a tax efficient structure for you and your family. We will work with you as your strategic tax partner, whether you wish to build a property investment portfolio or your medical business.

GUIDES

Property investors and medical professionals guides.

Property investors: Download our guide to building a tax efficient property investment business. Medical professionals: Download our business and tax guide to growing your practice.

www.optimiseaccountants.co.uk

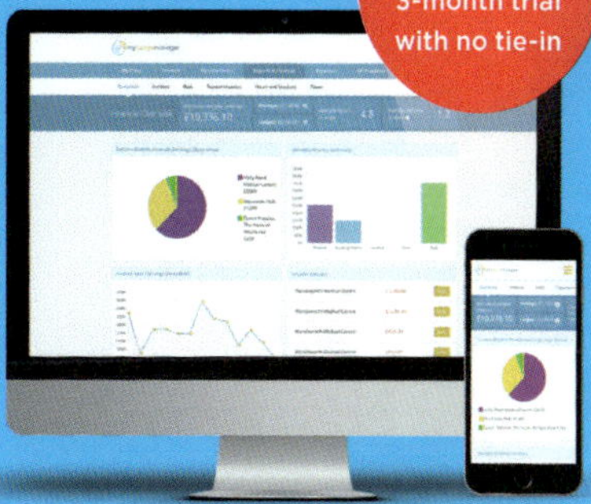

Six-Step Outsourcing Process

You can't be successful in business by doing everything yourself, especially if you trying to it alongside a busy medical career. Being able to effectively delegate your work in a reliable and efficient way an essential skill you need to master.

Hiring part-time help is easier and cheaper than ever. www.onlinejobs.ph gives you access to thousands of skilled, motivated and affordable Virtual Assistants (VA) in the Philippines. To hire freelancers from other countries, including the UK, you can try www.peopleperhour.com or www.upwork.com.

However, finding a VA is the easy part. What is more challenging is delegating tasks to your remote worker so they are able to do your work for you, exactly the way you want it done, without your constant involvement. Get this right, and your productivity will soar, get this wrong, and you can spend more time managing than it would have taken you to do it yourself!

Dr Steve Day from the Systems and Outsourcing company has put together The Six-Step Outsourcing PROCES™ to help you prioritise what work to outsource first, delegate it effectively and manage your remote workers efficiently.

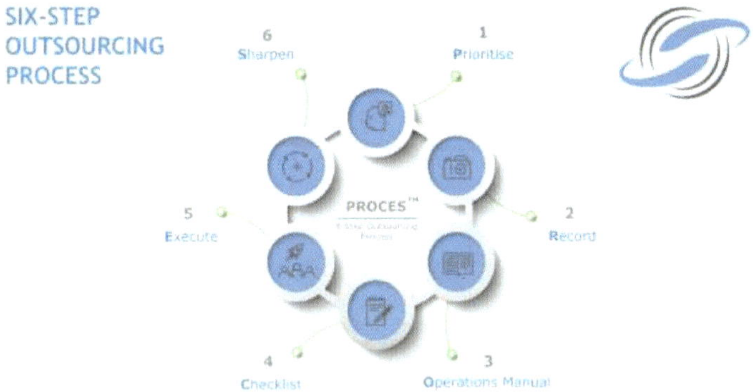

PRIORITISE: Step one is all about prioritising what you should be outsourcing. By delegating your time-consuming, simple tasks first, you will free up the most amount of time with the least amount of effort. These early wins will give you the encouragement and motivation to go on to systemise the rest of your business and free yourself completely from the day-to-day workings of your company. As a Eurekadoc reader, you can get free access to create your own Personal Systemisation Plan at http://s-a-o.uk/eurekadoc-psp

RECORD: In step two you'll learn how to Record your instructions in such a way that your VA can complete the task without any further input from you. For quick recordings, the Chrome plugin from https://www.useloom.com/ is free and easy to use. For longer videos and editing, https://screencast-o-matic.com/ is feature rich and really affordable and will scale with your team.

OPERATIONS MANUAL: Step 3 introduces your 'Operations Manual' which is your step-by-step, idiot-proof guide to carrying out every single process in your company. We'll talk about how you get other people to create this essential document for you. This a hugely time-consuming task and not one you should be taking on yourself as a business owner.

CHECKLIST: Step 4 is all about Checklists- something you as doctors should be very familiar with. However, most small business hardly uses them despite there effectiveness is getting multistep tasks completed correctly every time.

EXECUTION: Step 5 covers task delegation, communication with a remote team and workflow management. www.asana.com is a free and feature-rich task and project management tool. IT comes with a number of native plugins such as Harvest for time tracking and Instagantt for visual project management and team working.

SHARPEN: And lastly, in Step 6, you'll learn about creating a culture of continuous improvement within your business. Here you delegate the responsibility of improving your processes to the people who are actually doing the work for you.

You can find a free video series covering all 6 steps in detail at http://s-a-o.uk/eurekadoc-six-step

Medic Footprints
Where can your transferable skills take you today?
Connecting doctors.
Leveraging talent.
20% off membership MFEUDC
medicfootprints.org

Property and business education for doctors

Eurekadoc: https://www.eurekadoc.com/

In person courses: https://www.eurekadoc.com/courses

Online courses: https://www.eurekadoc.com/online-courses

Webinar library: https://www.eurekadoc.com/copy-of-online-courses

Books: https://www.eurekadoc.com/books

Coaching enquiries: property@eurekadoc.com

Property Investing for Doctors social media accounts

Facebook group: https://www.facebook.com/groups/100334890630082/

Instagram: @the_propertydoctor

Property sourcing

Pentagon property: https://www.pentagonproperty.co.uk/

Parachute properties: https://www.parachuteproperties.co.uk/

International property sourcing and services

Worldwide Property Co: https://worldwideproperty.co/

Mortgage finance for doctors

OnPoint Mortgages: https://www.onpointmortgages.com/

Access Financial Services: https://www.accessfs.co.uk/

Peer to peer lending and crowdfunding platforms

Blend Network: https://www.blendnetwork.com/

Simple Crowdfunding: https://www.simplecrowdfunding.co.uk/

Crowd With Us: https://www.crowdwithus.london/

Landlord accreditation organisations

National Landlord Association: https://landlords.org.uk/

Property management software

Landlord vision: https://www.landlordvision.co.uk/

Solicitors for conveyancing and lease extensions

Comptons: http://www.comptons.co.uk/

Solicitors for lease option, loan agreement and JV contracts

Miramar Legal: https://miramarlegal.co.uk/

MS Law: https://ms-law.co.uk/

Property accountants for doctors

Optimise Accountants: https://www.optimiseaccountants.co.uk/

Fylde Tax Accountants: http://www.fyldetaxaccountants.co.uk/

Locum work management software

My Locum Manager: https://mylocummanager.com/

Building and construction companies

17 Build: https://www.seventeenbuild.com/

Builder and tradespeople marketplace

Rated People: https://www.ratedpeople.com/

Check a trade: https://www.checkatrade.com/

My Builder: https://www.mybuilder.com/

Project management and quantity surveyor

https://www.redshell.org/

Planning consultancy

DRK Planning: https://www.drkplanning.co.uk/index.html

Architects

Formed Architects: https://formedarchitects.com/our-team/tina-patel/

Boom Studio: www.boomstudio.co

Ackroyd Lowrie: https://ackroydlowrie.com/

Interior design companies

Imtiaz Hussain Design: http://www.imtiazhussaindesigns.com/

Ademchic: https://www.ademchic.com/

DIY lettings and sales portals (i.e. self-managed property listings)

Openrent: https://www.openrent.co.uk/

Upad: https://www.upad.co.uk/

Purplebricks: https://www.purplebricksplc.com/

DIY room lets portals

Easy roommate: https://uk.easyroommate.com/

Spareroom: https://www.spareroom.co.uk/

Serviced accommodation and holiday let listings

Airbnb: https://www.airbnb.co.uk/

Booking.com: https://www.booking.com/

Home Away: https://www.homeaway.co.uk/

Channel management software

Kigo: https://www.kigo.net/

Key collection solutions

Keybox system: https://www.keyboxsystems.com/

Key Nest: https://keynest.com/

Serviced accommodation services

Hostmaker: https://hostmaker.com/gb/

Air Sorted: https://www.airsorted.uk/

Outsourcing

Fiverr: https://www.fiverr.com/

Upwork: https://www.upwork.com/

Onlinejobs.ph: https://www.onlinejobs.ph/

Project management and team communication apps

Basecamp: https://basecamp.com/

Asana: https://asana.com/

Trello: https://trello.com/

Slack: https://slack.com/

Housing charities

Shelter: https://www.shelter.org.uk/

Land Aid: https://www.landaid.org/

Crisis: https://www.crisis.org.uk/

Mind: https://www.mind.org.uk/

Doctor wellbeing charities

Financial help for doctors and their families: https://www.doctorshelp.org.uk/

Diverse careers and wellness for doctors

Medic Footprints: https://medicfootprints.org/

NHS Clinical Entrepreneur Programme: https://www.england.nhs.uk/ourwork/innovation/clinical-entrepreneur/

APPENDIX: TERMINOLOGY

ABBREVIATIONS

A&E: accident and emergency department
BMV: below market value
BOE: Bank of England
BTL: buy to let
CCG: Clinical Commissioning Group
CGT: Capital Gains Tax
ERC: early redemption charge
F1/F2: foundation year doctor (year 1 or year 2)
FCA: Financial Conduct Authority
FTB: first time buyer
GDV: gross development value
GMC: General Medical Council
GP: general practice or general practitioner
HMO: house of multiple occupation
HMRC: Her Majesty's Revenue and Customs
HNWI: high net worth individual
IFA: independent financial advisor
IHT: Inheritance Tax
ISA: individual savings account
IT: Income Tax
LO: lease option
LTV: loan to value
NHS: National Health Service
PLO: purchase lease option
PO: purchase option
R2R: rent to rent
ROCE: return on capital employed
ROCI: return on capital invested

ROI: return on investment
SA: serviced accomodation
SDLT: Stamp Duty Land Tax
SIPP: self-invested personal pension
sqft: square feet
sqm: square meters
SSTC: sold subject to contract
ST: specialist trainee doctor (ranges from Year 1 to Year 8)

DEFINITIONS

Buy-to-let: buying a property to rent it out

Buy-to-flip: buying a property to sell

Buy-refurbish-refinance (to release capital): buying a property, refurbishing it to increasing it and re-financing it to release the profits you have generated. Bear in mind that the funds released to you by the bank is 'debt'.

Developments: developing a property through refurbishment or re-structure or building it from the ground up

Build to sell schemes: Building properties to sell afterwards

Rent-to-rent: renting a property with permission to sublet

Multi-lets: renting a property to multiple tenants

Purchase lease options: a contractual agreement which gives the investor the right to purchase a property at an agreed price, within a given time period without the obligation to do so

Serviced accommodation: property that is offered with addition services such as guest check-in, laundry, cleaning

Build-to-rent: Building properties to hold and rent to tenants

Social housing: affordable housing for people on low incomes or other needs

Care homes: residential homes providing care and support for people (the type of care may vary depending on the needs of the individuals)

Title splitting: splitting a single dwelling property into two or more properties to rent out or sell

Commercial conversions: converting commercial premises such as offices into residential properties

ABOUT THE AUTHOR

Lafina Diamandis is a doctor, educator and property investor with over ten years of experience buying, developing and selling residential properties in the UK. She purchased her first property in 2008 just after the UK recession struck (an ideal time to buy!) but her eye-opening experience came a few years later through helping a relative to source and refurbish a property in central London –she created over £100,000 value in only six weeks.

Inspired by the creativity, entrepreneurship and financial independence that can be experienced in property, Lafina set out to learn as much as possible about property investment and the strategies used. This resulted in her building a portfolio of projects, including some which required no financial investment of her own. Her desire to help other doctors and healthcare professionals understand property investment (whether it be to help with the process of a first-time purchase or build up their own property portfolio) was the motivation for writing this book.

Inspired by her own diverse career path and the desire to help other doctors do the same, Lafina founded Eurekadoc Publishing to provide niche career guides for doctors. This later evolved into Eurekadoc, a social enterprise co-founded by herself and Aroon Baskaradas to give doctors the tools and resources they need to create the career and lifestyle they desire through diverse medical education and insightful careers design. Eurekadoc provides webinars, courses, virtual learning and books to support the career development and interests of the twenty-first century doctor. This means focusing on much-neglected topics such as business and finance and health and wellness, as well as hot topics in healthcare!

Lafina has a passion for teaching and has delivered education and training to over a thousand doctors to date. She is an advocate for portfolio careers in medicine and is the author of two books.

Her desire is to help doctors to understand property investment and make educated decisions, whether buying their first home or investing in their own GP surgery or health premises. One of her dreams is to make it possible for any healthcare professional to invest in great property projects for as little as £1,000 and with full transparency. In May 2018 this dream came true when her first property crowdfunding project known as The Doctors' Project was overfunded in just seven minutes! Look out for more in the pipeline.

Having a career spanning clinical medicine, research, entrepreneurship and investment. she realised she was best suited to a portfolio career that allowed her to leverage and utilise her business skills within medicine. As a result, she approaches her work with more passion and purpose than ever before and feels a sense of fulfilment and satisfaction that she did not believe to be possible. In 2017, Lafina was offered a place on the NHS Clinical Entrepreneur Programme, the largest programme of its kind in the world supporting innovation in healthcare. Here she has continued growing Eurekadoc and is working on ambitious housing projects with social impact.

Currently working on a pipeline of developments between £1 and £5 million across the UK, Lafina's focus is on leveraging her experience and contacts in both real estate and healthcare, to create innovative solutions for housing problems faced by patients as well as healthcare staff. She is motivated by projects with a social purpose and is curious about how concepts such as co-living can be used within the healthcare sphere, and the bio-psycho-social impact this could have on our communities.

Lafina is regularly asked to speak and hold workshops at events all over the UK and is on the Membership Committee for Qandor Property Developers Club. She was recently featured on the Nicole Bremner Property podcast discussing the overlap between her interests in healthcare and real estate. Lafina loves to connect with like-minded people so if you would like to get involved in property projects with a social impact, drop her a line at property@eurekadoc.com or you can follow her for brick tips or posts on the relationship between health and housing at:

Instagram @the_propertydoctor

LinkedIn: https://www.linkedin.com/in/dr-lafina-diamandis-487b5bb1/

Facebook: https://www.facebook.com/The-Property-Doctor-181603859055165/

Closed Facebook group: https://www.facebook.com/groups/100334890630082/

ACKNOWLEDGEMENTS

First, I want to start by thanking my mother and father, to whom I owe everything! We have certainly not come from a family of property developers but Mam, your first refurb in the dashing colours of lime green and orange and Dad, your humble beginnings renting a tiny windowless room in Bayswater back in the seventies, are examples I will always carry with me. Your stories, struggles and achievements have always motivated and inspired me to do my best and never give up when things get tough. Thank you for your infinite love and support, and massive thanks to my Mam for painstakingly editing this book! Next I give thanks to my sister, who so generously allowed me to refurbish (experiment) on her flat during the early days—thank you for trust and your love! To my partner Sifis for over a decade of friendship and for supporting me with snacks, laughs and massages after hours on the computer—I'm so grateful! To my wider family and my dear friends who helped me to follow my dreams, supported me in every endeavour (yes, even when painting flats or moving furniture at midnight!) and encouraged me to write this book, I could not have achieved half of my goals if it weren't for your continuous encouragement, support and understanding.

My thanks to the following amazing doctors who generously shared their personal experiences of property investment in the case studies featured throughout the book: Say Vivekanantham; Louise Hancock; Rahul Sahay; Zoe Malik-Kemp; William Gao; Rachael Coates; Cat Davison; John Friis, and Steve Day. It has been a great joy to get to know other doctors who share my passion for property and an honour to hear and to publish each of your unique stories in this book.

A big thank you to Simon Misiewicz from Optimise Accountants who wrote the tax chapter and who has been a big supporter of

Eurekadoc from the beginning. Thank you, Simon, for your ongoing contributions to the community through our Facebook group, courses and webinars, and for the invaluable tax advice for doctors you continue to share. Thanks also goes to Lee Langley from OnPoint Mortgages and to Sofoclis Patsalosavvis at Seventeen Build who I interviewed as part of my research for this book and whose tips, advice and recommendations have been invaluable. Thank you to Dylan Mitchell from Worldwide Properties for his kind tips and advice for doctors thinking of buying abroad, and of course to my friends and colleagues at Qandor Property Developers Club who have encouraged, supported and held me accountable over the last year.

Special thanks to the Eurekadoc team who have supported and encouraged me to write this book, and to my co-founder and dear friend Aroon Baskaradas for helping me to create the space to finish it at last! Thank you, buddy. I couldn't have done it without you! Thanks to Polly Sullivan, Alex Ganzerla, Professor Tony Young and our colleagues on the NHS Clinical Entrepreneur Programme for their support and encouragement. I thank my best friend Tinni Guha Roy for her help with the book launch, I couldn't have done it without you! We're also immensely grateful for the support of our friends and long-term promotion partners at Medic Footprints, My Locum Manager and Doctors.net. It has been a great pleasure to support and see each other grow over the last few years and we look forward to continuing to do so! Thanks to Richard McMunn and team who also inspired me to write my own book and from whom I learnt the process of self-publishing. I am so grateful for your support and advice. I would also like to thank my editor Kim Farnell and my many friends and colleagues who took the time to proofread my book and give me feedback: Khyati Shah; Rebecca Casey; Pooja Arora; Abeyna Jones and Nigel Giam.

Last but not least, thanks to the following doctors, who contributed to the research phase of the book by offering their suggestions for topics of interest. This helped me ensure the book was as relevant to doctors as possible and I hope you will find the content as useful as your suggestions have been to me! Heartfelt thanks to: Adefolake Adeyemi Yusuff; Aisha Conviver; Ajay Karigi; Bennett Alakakone; Bilal Khan; Catherine Austin; Claire Merrifield; Deniah Pachai; Denise O'Hanlon; Fairoz Miller; Hannah Nazri; Iram Ali; Kunal Khanna; Laura Stafford; Mark Riley; Matt Rickard; Mehdi Noori; Mohsin Khan; Paul Moutray; Paul Williams; Rachael Frances; Ravina Bhanot; Sarah Goulding; Tang Chiu Yau and Thomas Perkins. To everyone else who may have contributed to this book and to my experiences in property, I thank you from the bottom of my heart.

18018367R00111

Printed in Great Britain
by Amazon